ERP
Lessons Learned
Structured Process

Wayne L. Staley

Cover designed by: Phase Four Graphics LL

Copyright © 2014 by Affinity Systems LLC

ISBN-13:9781482035551

ISBN-10: 1482035553

Dedications

This book dedicated to Jerry Martin, now riding his "hog" with James Dean and Jack Kerouac on the highways of heaven.

Contents

Introduction

ERP Lessons Learned - Structured Process presents a Nine Step method to translate business into software definitions, then evaluate, purchase and install ERP system solutions.

One of the lessons learned is thinking in systems terms. A business is a collection of systems that must work in harmony to produce a successful result. A new system may optimize efforts in one functional system, while introducing greater complexity in others.

In today's manufacturing world, resource management has an all-inclusive definition, extending beyond planning requirements for materials, labor, and machines.

Traditionally, ERP projects avoid implementing process improvement programs while evaluating and installing software systems. In this book, they are dependent components to resource planning and optimization. The information systems are highways for enabling change, facilitating process improvement. Planned as one system, but implemented in two stages, they work in concert.

This concept has expanded to include virtually every resource in the organization, planned as one overall system.

Since its inception, ERP has grown steadily more complicated, robust, and expensive to purchase and install. Comprehensive systems are still available but new approaches provide industry with advanced and in some cases, more simplified solutions, including cloud applications, modularity, and a return to the simple functionality of MRP.

Rethinking ERP/MRP will result in exciting expanded applications for achieving excellence in the new world of manufacturing. This book is a structured process written as a guide to a successful ERP journey.

Foreword

Fellow traveler on the ERP journey,

ERP projects are tough but important projects for the future of your company. Competitive pressures will only intensify, and companies must perform at ever-faster speeds. Issues of sustainability and resource conservation are gaining importance, and intensifying the need for contemporary ERP systems.

The message to executive management is uncomplicated. Due diligence at the very start of the program often determines the result. Invest the appropriate time defining the business direction, and never short-cut training. ERP is a top-down matching process, and imprecision increases at each level of detail. Given the buildup of variance, the software may bear little resemblance to the desired strategy, resulting in a system incompatible with future business needs.

Carefully select team members, provide training, and trust your team. Avoid taking shortcuts, especially for training. Last, you must stay involved and be willing to take action if the program bogs down.

Those associates serving as project team members, directly or on functional teams, will significantly contribute to business effectiveness, and influence many lives. Situations will not always reflect reality, so stay alert, and never let your guard down. Ask the tough questions and demand answers from software suppliers, other team members, and fellow workers. Quality is important. Establish high standards and challenge yourself and others to achieve them. When the project is performing successfully, all will celebrate their quality contributions.

To everyone in the organization - a successful project result is a positive for you and fellow workers. Associates will grow in knowledge and importance to both current and perhaps future organizations. From a broad business perspective, the company can run faster, more effectively, and better service customers, providing more jobs and opportunities for advancement.

We dedicated this book to Jerry, a friend, worker, and builder, a stonemason that spent his life mortaring rough and oddly shaped stones into beautiful structures. He understood that people, like stones, are different sizes, shapes and strength, but working together they produce a beautiful and lasting result.

Take pride in your work and enjoy the ERP journey.

Wayne Staley
Affinity Systems LLC

Acknowledgements

We thank the following persons: Natalie Groshek Staley, Scott Guenther, Jon Bingol, Lisa Guenther, and Angela Bernsten.

Overview

Businesses must compete within constraints such as capital formation, growth, automation, governmental regulation, and global competition. In addition to these constraints, they must address economic circularity concerns dealing with sustainability, resource availability, yield, carbon footprints, and repurposed materials and waste. This has become a pervasive, corporate-wide endeavor.

Competition is about speed, quality, adaptability, and productivity. This includes product availability, customer service, manufacturing, supply chains, and decision-making. The faster industry moves the more information sensitive it becomes. As velocity increases, the information stream must retain high levels of integrity and provide actionable data in real time.

Enterprise Resource Planning (ERP) systems are the information super highways for adaptive and agile processes, but they are expensive to justify, prepare for, install, and use. The expanding cloud options bring the power of ERP to virtually every type and size of enterprise.

Information and intelligence are half of the equation. The other half is flexible and adaptive production processes that can swiftly respond to threats and/or opportunities. This requires automation, real-time proficiency, and active fast-paced process improvement programs, managed by information at the speed of reality.

Lean Six Sigma improves processes in the physical world, where people, energy, time, and materials converge. Ideally, processes travel within the constraints of the integrated formal system instead of unstructured informal processes. Continuous improvement provides the tools to accelerate business processes on the information super highway.

To compete, companies must have contemporary systems facilitating perpetual time compression, cutting every type of waste, and capable of real-time interaction in a connected global marketplace.

The life cycles for many ERP and Lean Six Sigma programs are approaching final stages where they also become constraints. New and better approaches are available, that incorporate the above key issues.

ERP and process improvement programs complement and support each other, but compete for resources. While ERP is dramatically changing, it remains the core planning and control system, overlaying the physical realities of the production systems. Process improvement is for the hard, practical world where work methods have to be improved. The physical and informational perspectives are important considerations when performing any needs assessment and planning a future state.

This book is about selecting and installing modern ERP systems, forming the evidence-based foundation needed to achieve unrivaled success. To realize that purpose, the forces reshaping business and information integration need review.

Systems within Systems

Any enterprise is a complex cause and effect system comprised of subordinate complex systems and cycles. The search for business solutions, be it software, process improvement, or some other approach, must address these total systems relationships. Addressing one specific area, such as the production process, has consequences in all the other systems. Products may require reengineering to fit new processes. Capability affects what product availability. Waste factors and energy consumption calculations aid process improvement.

The following chart, Business Dependencies - I/O, shows the enterprise structure broken into input/process/output functions. The purpose is to visualize the activities in the nine-step selection and implementation process. Optimized systems provide competitive opportunities. We term this business at the speed of reality, synchronizing the speed of information, processes, and intelligent response. The chart is comprised of four segments.

Strategy

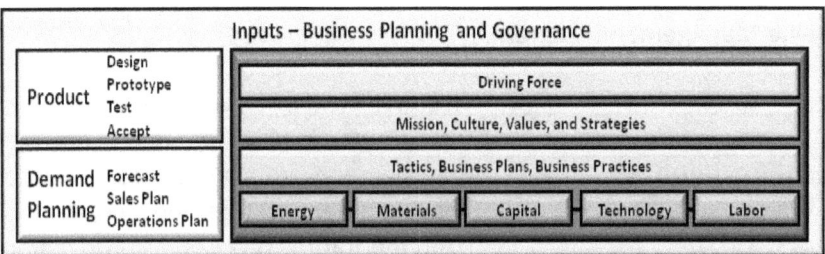

The highest level is strategy. This consists of Business planning and governance, defining the direction, designing the products, and acquiring the needed assets to buy/make the product. Making key decisions about where and how to manufacture product and acquiring the capital to put plans into action are strategic

Value Adding Operations I/P/O

The second level consists of value-adding activities including customer order processing, resource planning, procurement, manufacturing, production output, distribution, and fulfillment.

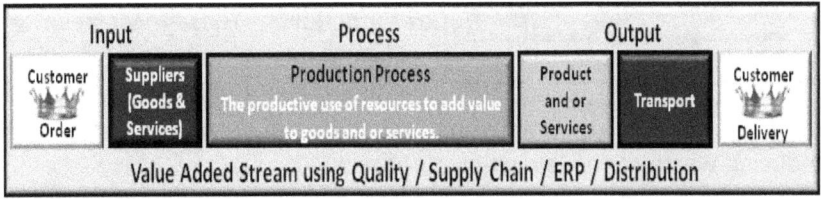

Resource Waste Issues

The third level is comprised of built-in activities resulting in waste, a natural part of any business processes. These include process waste, financial issues, and time utilization. Managing these waste streams through continuous process improvement programs increases resource yield, lowers cost, increases profits, and reduces negative environmental footprints. These are broken into three segments: waste, financial, and time.

Value Management Programs

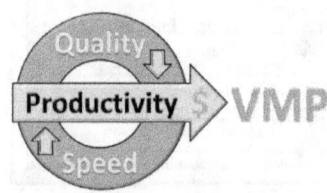

Value Management Program

The first symbol is VMP. Business must take responsibility for resource management, from an ethical, business image, and financial perspective, through contemporary process improvement (Value Management Programs) where the intent is to add value to every task performed, and resource used. From our perspective, quality is the common thread, and doing the wrong thing faster will always be a losing strategy. For this book, the acronym VMP encompasses quality, process improvement, transformation process, and value added concepts. Lean, short for Lean Six Sigma, appears where appropriate.

Process Waste

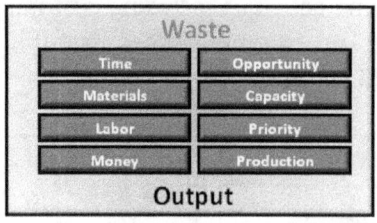

Process waste is the second block, addressing time, materials, labor, opportunity, capacity, priority, and production. These wastes are unavoidable, a natural part of any process. Every effort must focus on yield, which is getting the most value out of every resource, while reducing waste to the lowest levels possible.

The following chart breaks waste down another level, and illustrates the expansion of the process improvement concept, normally confined to the block labeled "Process Improvement Targets," but today, inclusive of all process waste.

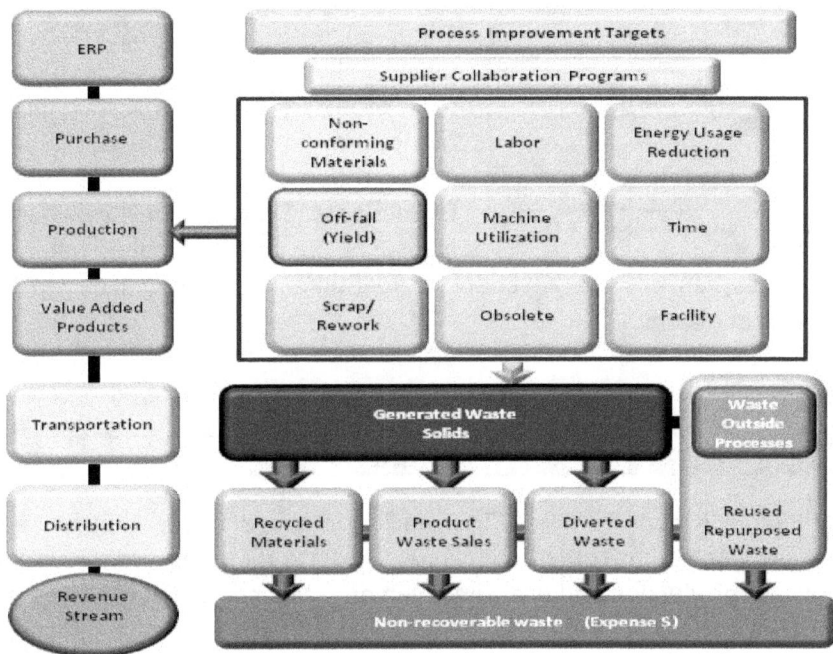

Those issues shown under the labels Generated Waste Solids and Waste outside Processes have become opportunities for financial, environmental, and regulatory purposes.

Many companies have expanded process improvement teams, actively finding methods to convert waste products into profits or other resources. One example is co-generation, where heat waste is converted into energy and/or hot water, feeding other systems. Other companies are finding methods to repurpose materials, such as manufacturing residual, to sell as secondary products, thereby converting waste into revenue streams.

The concept of zero inventories now incorporates zero wastes. Keep each of these issues in mind while working through the process.

Financial

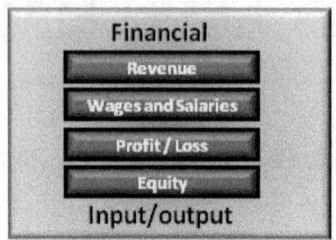

Third, all business systems affect the financial health of the business, cash flow, profits, growth, and sustainability. Money may not buy happiness or fulfill a personal passion, but it is the lifeblood for business. Every business constantly measures the financial pulse, but new systems can provide a variety of real-time information to augment decision-making.

Time

The fourth level is time. Time and money are finite, fungible, and exchangeable but compete in value. We state the time/money cycle as instant production and use. Time elements expanding that fundamental metric contain potential for improvement, but are subject to the law of diminishing returns.

Every activity takes time, and time is not just money; it is opportunity and risk. The faster you drive the business cycle the greater the ability to take advantage of opportunities, meet priorities, and manage cash flow. Speed has consequences, increasing the risk of mismatches and errors. It is useful to develop a design of experiment mentality, quickly reacting when results fail to meet the plan.

The following chart puts each topic in perspective.

Business-dependencies – I/O

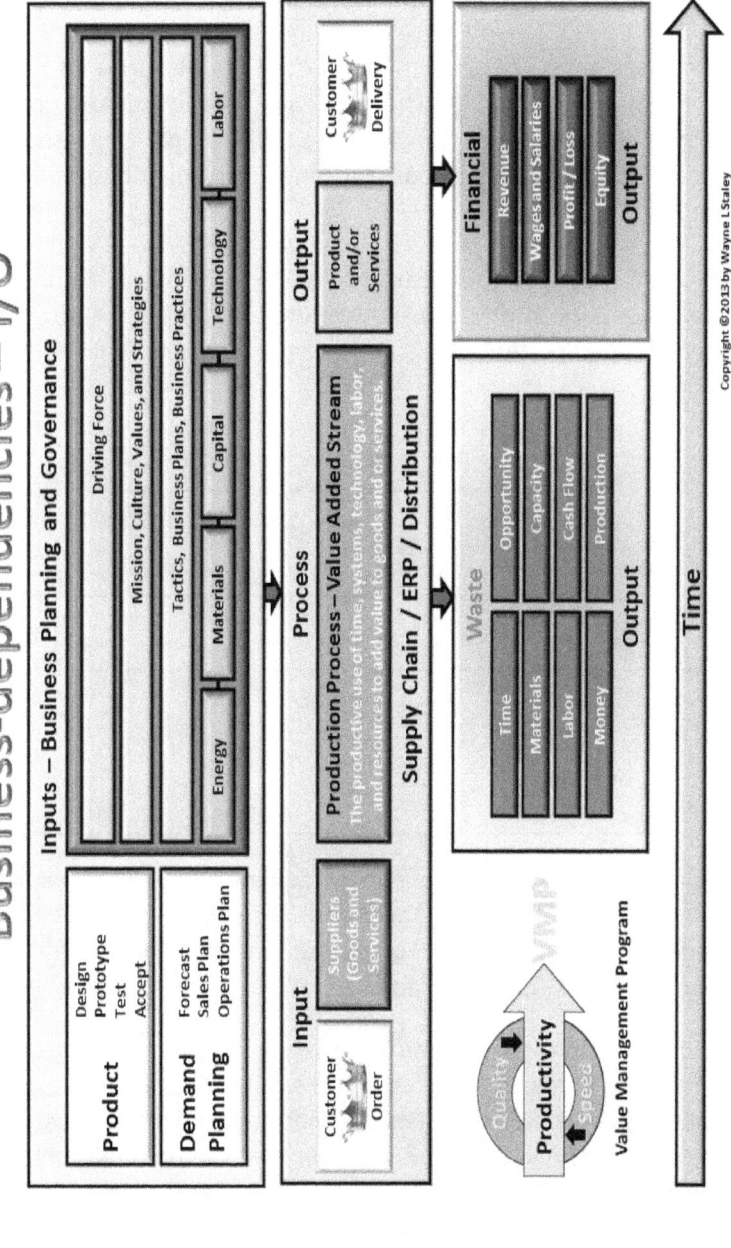

7

Closed Loop ERP System

The Closed-Loop ERP System translates the enterprise into information technology terminology. The objective is to find and implement a system providing core functions capable of planning and managing resources, engineering, production, inventory, distribution, and financial systems.

As a reminder, at the heart of MRP/ERP beats a simple, relational calculation. The method uses demand, as forecasts and/or orders, to calculate requirements.

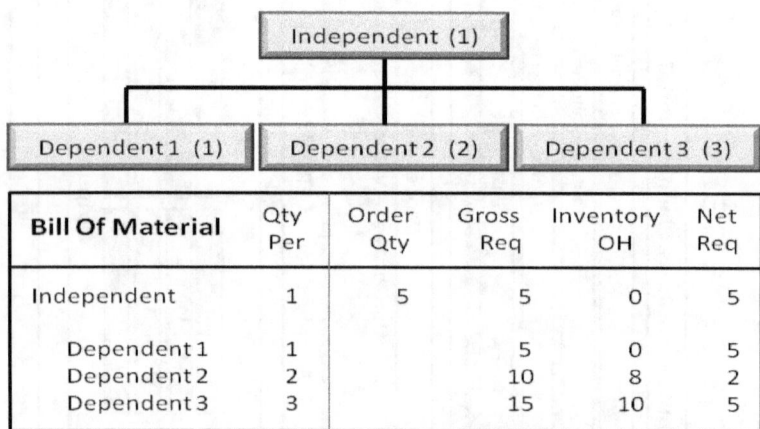

Bill Of Material	Qty Per	Order Qty	Gross Req	Inventory OH	Net Req
Independent	1	5	5	0	5
Dependent 1	1		5	0	5
Dependent 2	2		10	8	2
Dependent 3	3		15	10	5

The independent order quantity (demand) is multiplied against the quantity per for each dependent component to calculate gross requirements, in turn netted against inventory to calculate how many dependent parts are required to produce the independent order.

This calculation is the same for making cars or oatmeal cookies. The complexity increases by extending this simple calculation to incorporate other dependencies such as time, machines, labor, energy, and money. When new, the label was RRP, Relational Requirements Planning, and incorporated in modeling systems. The early gurus, Oliver Wight, Joseph Orlicky, Walter E Goddard, and George Plossl continued to develop the system through multiple iterations of sophistication, labeled MRP,

MRPII, and finally ERP. The closed-loop concept on the next page is their work, and it is still the core of ERP systems.

Modern ERP systems provide capabilities far beyond this simple chart, as discussed in detail throughout the book. The overall value of the system still rests with the quality and user-friendly performance of the core software functionality.

From this chart, it becomes obvious that MRP/ERP systems are transaction intensive. Given the proliferation of information technology, every evaluation must consider how to effectively capture and disburse information. A company may employ the most sophisticated software in the world, but unless information is managed, timely, accurate, and complete, the system serves little purpose.

Closed Loop ERP System
Information Flow

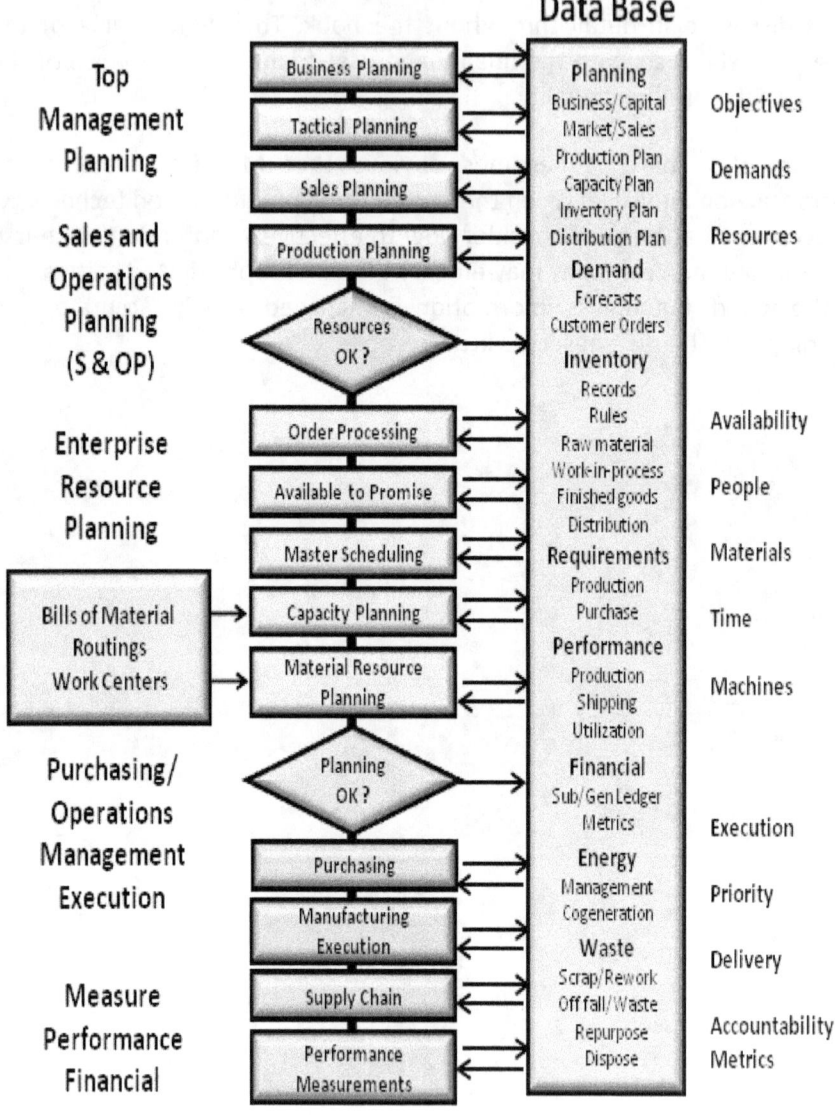

Copyright©2014 Wayne L Staley

10

The Project Objective

Business must build adaptive, flexible, and resource-efficient systems operating at the speed of reality. This translates into enlightened governance, contemporary ERP systems, productive process improvement programs, optimized resources, and highly interactive and collaborative supply chains.

As you start this project, remember that success means understanding exactly how these elements work and affect each other. You want to make the organization very efficient, but the ultimate objective is for the system to provide controlled speed, with every element of the enterprise working in sync. The rule is "efficiency never trumps effectiveness." An effective ERP system enables the process improvements needed to gain velocity, but not at the expense of increased process waste or reduced quality.

Time and time management are/must be priorities in both planning and execution. ERP projects will steal time if not specifically and tightly managed. At the same time, it is important to provide the time needed to facilitate a quality ERP outcome.

Decision Process

Executive management and the project team will make hundreds of decisions throughout the project. This chart is from the Affinity Systems LLC training program, "Decision Support,"

Evaluate every ERP and process improvement program on its own merits, and walk through each step. When evaluating current programs, the last two steps are essential.

Decision Process

Program Assessment

Establish a program selection team. Perform due diligence (needs assessment) and program evaluation (ability to meet the needs).

- Strategies - know what you want to do and why
- Learn how to do it
- Uncompromising focus on "doing what is right"
- Structure project to avoid or eliminate power conflicts and unnecessary approval processes
- Manage the egos
- Develop a reward and recognition system so players have a stake in the game
- Define who will manage the program and how they will be held accountable
- Rigorously follow-up on implementation progress

Constraints and Criticality

Determine program criticality to achieving your business mission and goals. If criticality/priority is low, it rapidly increases the probability for failure. Consider scrapping or postponing the initiative until internal conflicts are resolved. Define potential constraints and think through solutions. Review all governance issues.

Information

Integrate information technology and Lean programs into all planning activities. Establish the parameters needed for program evaluation. Obtain information from all the program suppliers, both in-house and consulting companies. Define which computer systems require modification to support the program. Establish metrics and data capture methods. Determine feedback mechanisms to executive management. Establish informational meetings to update the organization on progress. Consider using visual methods and post results throughout the organization. While an internal newsletter keeps people informed, splashy displays get more attention.

Recommendations and Options

Assign a project leader. Make sure there is a detailed plan. Think through the program organization. Detail the relevance of each element and training approach.

The project team is required to compile a program comparison, assessing the merits and the options each provides. Dollarize every option on this list with a projected cost and return on investment (ROI).

Select a Project Management Methodology

A program methodology keeps the team members involved, using similar documents and methods to tighten communications. There are many project management methodologies, including Agile, Change Management, Lean Six Sigma, Total Quality Management, and Waterfall. We present a method titled ACTION, in Step 9 Continuous Improvements - Perfect the System.

Select a Project Management Program

The use of a project management program such as Microsoft Project is highly recommended. Larger software companies such as SAP and Epicor have project management modules. There are a number of programs available, including open source, cloud Aps, or the company intranet, while providing mobile views of the information. Key among them is the individual task list. Several team members must learn how to establish, maintain, and use the program. Spreadsheet programs can get the job done, but they are time-consuming, less effective, and difficult to share. Evaluate the options and choose a package. It should minimally provide:

- Scheduling - calendar management, task, resources, time, and assignments
- Time management - including PERT, Critical path, calculations and visualization
- Activity reporting - online, mobile
- Team collaboration
- Change management functionality

Impact on Missions and Goals

The executive staff, presented with the finding from the project team, must question how each option affects the mission and business operations. Are they cost-effective and business-centric? Can the unintended consequences' decrease quality of service or operation? Are the resources available to fund the program? Does the system facilitate growth and operational efficiency?

Make the Decision

Given all the facts and data, carefully think through the entire business initiative. Have you covered the bases? Does it pass all the financial concerns? Is there passion for the program? Do you trust the project leaders and consultants? Are the associates on board with the project? Make the decision but include checkpoints, specific provisions, and constraints. Continued program oversight is required.

Implement the Program

Complete a detailed implementation plan. Leadership must carefully put each program stage into effect.
- Form the team
- Train the people
- Provide tools, resources and support to the team
- Hold teams "accountable" for their actions or inactions

Give the program a grand kickoff meeting. Go for it with gusto. A tepid approach will receive a weak response. You want the program to ring with the theme from Rocky, "Gonna Fly Now," or another inspirational music like "Eye of the Tiger." You bet this is show biz, and it absolutely builds excitement. If leadership does not demonstrate passion, why should the associates? Implement the program and make sure all metrics are in place and used.

Measure and Evaluate Progress

Measure all activities and correlate them to the project list. Is the program achieving the desired results on time and with high quality? Ask everyday/every week – are we on time, if not why not and how do we get back on track?

Corrective Action If Needed

The fault is not making errors; it is not catching them while small and taking corrective action. The entire team, if appropriately involved, will monitor and guide the program to a successful state.

ERP Selection Method

Every project needs a structured process, but many ERP projects reinvent one, instead of using a tested methodology. It helps to have a hardcopy with check off lists, as this one does.

The selection of ERP and/or process improvement programs can take different directions because both process and events drive actions. The chart and checklist may not be inclusive for your implementation.

Following is our method, customized for each project.

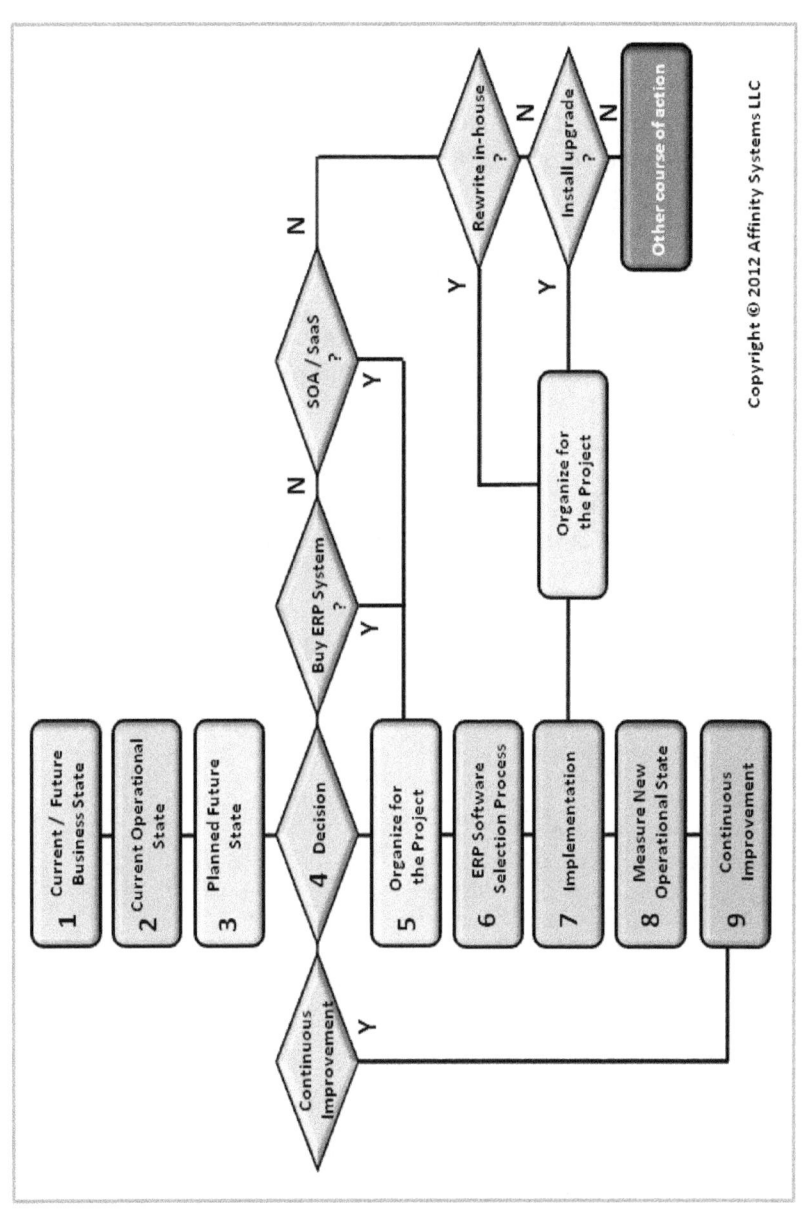

Illustration -ERP Project Chart

This process has nine sharply delineated steps.

1. Current/Future Business state
2. Current Operational State
3. Planned Future State
4. Decision
5. Organize for the Project
6. ERP Software Selection Process
7. Implementation
8. Measure New Operational State
9. Continuous Improvement/standardize

The checklists focus on the critical steps, and serves as a structured guide.

We, at Affinity Systems LLC, wish everyone success with their ERP journey.

Step 1 Current / Future Business State

Strategic planning is the first step of due diligence leading to the ERP selection and implementation process. There are multiple ways to analyze and synthesize a strategic direction, but the objective is a clear, stated direction forming the first premise layer for the business systems. This statement is the starting point for an iterative GAP analysis process.

Strategy formation evokes mixed emotions with executives. Premised on today's business variables, a status quo position is dangerous, given the disruptive forces at work in the global economy and speed of technological advancement. Given the dynamics of change, strategic planning should be an ongoing process, not a static event scheduled annually. One truth is clear. Strategy belongs to the President/CEO, Executive staff, and the Board of Directors.

In the book "The Art of War," Sun Tzu (ca. 500 BC) states: "Strategy without tactics is the slowest route to victory. Tactics without strategy is the noise before defeat."

Sun Tzu may have lived 2500 years ago, but he clearly understood you must know what war to fight before deciding how to fight it, who to lead the effort, who the troops will be and what resources to acquire and deploy.

The second definition is more humorous, but no less significant. While attributed to many speakers and authors, the core originator is the Cheshire cat, from Alice in Wonderland.

"If you don't know where you are going, any road will get you there."

A frequent comeback is "If you don't know where you are going, how will you know when you arrive?"

These quotes eloquently summarize the need for strategic planning. ERP and VMP programs require defined and documented business objectives. Failure to perform this core step instantly jeopardizes potential ERP projects. It is interesting that implementation project documents show time consuming, mind numbing detail. Follow-up is in brutal detail with verbal admonition for missing scheduled tasks. Conversely, getting a one or two-page strategic plan is often difficult. If a plan is not available, it means that executive management is:

- ☐ Uncertain where to direct the business
- ☐ Afraid to communicate it to the organization
- ☐ Concerned that competitors will use it for counter strategies

Products and product development must be included in the evaluation. The move to make niche or special products faster will continue to change business processes. Consequently, the specifics of the ERP package may vary. ERP or VMP must have precise documented direction, provided by the strategic exercise, or risk failure.

Documented strategies must be available very early in the process, and if not, consider delaying actions committing to a specific course of action. A company must know what program to do, plan and fund the project, and have clear goals.

Strategic Planning Process

As seen in the following illustration, the strategic planning process may be complex and time consuming. From an ERP project perspective, there are multiple important output requirements from the process.

1. An unambiguous strategy statement translated into information technology terms.

2. Document the detail of each strategy to enable the development of meaningful future states.
3. The outcome must identify all types of changes influencing the ERP functional requirements.
4. Establish the requirement to implement a needs assessment program.

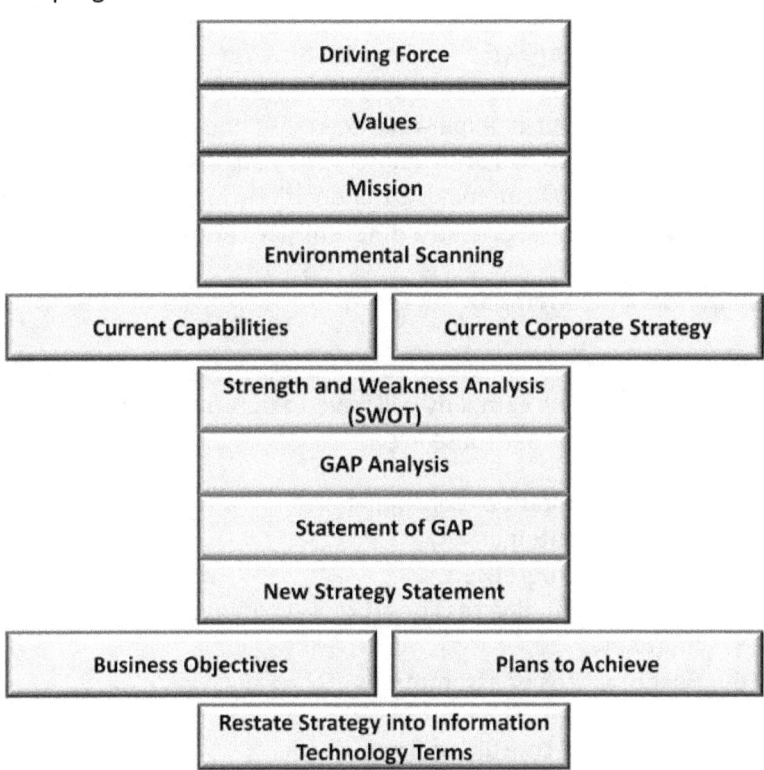

Few companies will execute a full-blown exercise, specifically for establishing the optimal direction needed before selecting an ERP system or VMP. Companies clearly understanding and articulating their direction have completed this step. Companies uncertain about future direction or unable to state their strategies must engage in planning at some positive level.

Planning Sequence

The appropriate planning sequence is top-down, starting with strategy, but some enterprises conduct and analyze the findings of the Current Operational State for input into the strategic planning process. After completing the business needs assessment, future operational strategies become increasingly obvious. The danger is bypassing the strategic planning analysis leading to broader changes in software functionality. If the decision is to perform a needs assessment without a strategy statement, it is imperative to revisit the issue before Step 3, developing the Planned Future State. This helps ensure a translatable strategy is in place before making the decisions in Step 4, to implement an ERP or VMP process, or take a different path altogether.

Strategic Planning Methods

There are a number of ways to conduct strategic planning, often interrelated, and each company will have to determine which method(s) best serve their purpose. These are:

1. Hire a consultant or consulting firm
2. Executive statement
3. Strategic conference
4. Intensive planning sessions (brain storming)
5. Interviews
6. Best practices or assumptions

Hire a consultant or consulting firm

Hire a consulting firm or consultant with strategic planning expertise and experience. Make sure:

- They understand your industry.
- They are experienced with strategies for your type of industry.
- Focus as facilitators and explore all issues.
- They are unaffiliated with an ERP supplier.

Executive Statement

Develop a strategy by proclamation. The President/CEO dictates the direction to the executive staff and provides a go/no go decision for conducting the current state operational study. If the strategies are translatable, the purpose is accomplished.

Strategic conference

The strategic conference is a traditional full-blown planning session. The executive staff isolates themselves and establishes where the company needs to go. Excellent tools are available for analyzing data on enterprise performance, product, marketplace, and customer feedback. In general, executive management knows if their customers are happy, if their products are competitive, and if their operations are efficient. Normal business metrics and financial reporting provide the basic intelligence to decide if the business is going in the right direction. A strategic conference normally involves or is the result of extensive research and intelligence gathering such as:

1. Feedback from customers
2. Business metrics and financial reports– what are they indicating
3. Capital investment requirements
4. Stockholder equity – goals and expectations
5. Competitive Advantage Analysis
6. Compensation plans
7. Strategic SWOT analysis (strengths, weaknesses, opportunities, and threats)
8. Growth plans/opportunities
9. Organizational responsibilities/assessments
10. Desired changes
11. Competitive technology assessment
12. Competitive products/ current product's comparison

These studies provide the intelligence to establish or modify business strategies and programs, including a new ERP or VMP. It may lead to a business transformation process, or need to modify the perception, behavioral characteristics, and actions of the people in the enterprise. To be of value, the process must convert the perceptions and needs identified into implementable strategies, objectives, and business plans.

Map the current strategies against future direction to develop a Gap profile.

1. Business opportunities and associated risks
2. Increasing strengths and reducing weaknesses
3. Competitive analysis - implications
4. Gaps between capability and current objectives

Intensive Planning Sessions (Brain storming)

Intensive Planning sessions are powerful strategic planning tools. While understanding their business direction, it requires translation into software terms. Having an agreement among members of management on specific interpretations is important. One-day brainstorming or intensive planning sessions are excellent for developing strategies and definitions. They:

- Bring associates together to focus on core issues
- Greatly condense the amount of time required for the planning activity
- Are highly interactive, causing tough problems to surface
- An excellent opportunity to discover how individuals think and if they agree with strategies

The executive staff, selected board members, leader of the operational state study and the consultant normally attends meetings. A consultant with strategic planning expertise will bring a fresh perspective and ask questions relevant to business direction. The result will be a greater number of options or expansion of current ones.

The intensive planning session works to gain buy in, support the strategies, and insures all the issues are on the table.

Interview

There are times when interviewing the executive staff as part of the business needs assessment is the only method that works.

- ☐ Interview all members of the executive staff
- ☐ Interview directors
- ☐ Compile and analyze strategies.
- ☐ Synthesize into strategic statements
- ☐ Executive approval
- ☐ Restate into ERP features

Interviews take place in conjunction with intensive planning sessions, or prior to an executive agreement.

Best practices or assumed strategies

The application of best practice or assumed strategies is the worst method for obtaining strategies. This involves literally restating obvious business goals. Following is a partial compilation of presumed strategies.

Our strategic direction will be:

- ☐ World-class Customer Service
- ☐ Statement of Quality Standards
- ☐ Improved Business Intelligence
- ☐ Increased process flexibility
- ☐ Reduced waste
- ☐ High-velocity production throughput
- ☐ High-velocity order to cash cycle
- ☐ Improved asset management
- ☐ Corporate integration
- ☐ Adaptability
- ☐ Higher profit margins
- ☐ Improved productivity

☐   Integrated supply chains

The above entities are enlightening. What company does not want to improve in these areas? This particular list lacks clarity, excluding specifics such as mergers and acquisitions, growth, markets, competitive actions, process changes or product development, all statements supportable with action plans and tactics.

Presumption is a high-risk activity when dealing with strategy. The impact in the real world could lead to improper ERP selection or a poorly implemented VMP. Worse, poor strategy escapes into the marketplace, where it can profoundly affect the sustainability of the enterprise.

From our perspective, using best practice or assumed strategies is risky. If executive management is unwilling or unable to provide strategies, consider cancelling or delaying the program. Every subsequent project step will lack definitive specific relationship to business objectives. If you proceed, be warned, the consequence may be a failed implementation.

Strategic Planning Outputs

Depending upon the method and scope of the project, the result will be simple statements or comprehensive direction. These include capital projects, customer needs, product analysis, breakthrough strategy, the need for transformational processes facilitating change, manufacturing systems rationalization, supply chain integration and collaboration, increased flexibility, innovation, competitive advantage and operational reengineering.

For ERP purposes, the strategic planning process must result in:

☐   Business model validation
☐   Realistic strategies
☐   Restatement of vision and mission

- ☐ Achieve document matching current strategies to current capabilities
- ☐ Develop new strategies and the actions required to fill the gap between current and objective capability. These include acquiring additional capability, increased capital investments, or scale back strategies to meet current capabilities.
- ☐ Mobile technology strategies

From these studies, set business objectives for activities affecting needed functional ERP requirements:

- ☐ Financial objective
    - ☐ Investment strategy
    - ☐ Risk/opportunity assessment
    - ☐ Profit growth
    - ☐ Return on investment / assets
    - ☐ Least risks
    - ☐ Total cost management

Additional direction may also influence the ERP process

- ☐ Marketing (Customers)
    - ☐ Planned penetration percent – market share
    - ☐ Define areas of real or potential competitive advantage
    - ☐ Define areas of real or potential comparative advantage
    - ☐ Definition of current and future markets to serve
    - ☐ Definition of products required to service markets
    - ☐ Definition of strategic programs such as customer collaboration / demand pull
    - ☐ Statement of information technology requirements such as Customer Relationship Management Software, and/or business intelligence functionality
    - ☐ Sales growth
    - ☐ New product identification / introduction
    - ☐ Market niche growth

- [ ] Steps to make each interaction with customers a positive one
- [ ] Technological customer interfaces

- [ ] Product
    - [ ] Design for life cycle – production through recycle
    - [ ] Design for energy efficiency
    - [ ] Design for reparability
    - [ ] Design for manufacturability
    - [ ] Design for minimal environmental impact
    - [ ] Establish quality requirements
    - [ ] Flexibility of use
    - [ ] Adaptability
    - [ ] Functionality
    - [ ] Technological level

- [ ] Operations
    - [ ] Document changes to ETO, ATO or other core paradigm
    - [ ] Document current and requested capital expenditures and their impact on the information and operational systems
    - [ ] Document outsourcing plans
    - [ ] Systems capability to support the smart enterprise
    - [ ] State vertical horizontal or hybrid organization
    - [ ] State need for VMP
    - [ ] Document contingency plans for acquiring product
    - [ ] Document energy saving opportunities

- [ ] Order winners (from the APICS Systems and Technology Review Course)
    - [ ] Price
    - [ ] Quality
    - [ ] Delivery
    - [ ] Flexibility
    - [ ] Product design
    - [ ] Service

    ☐   Image (e.g. green)

☐ Following are expectations from the strategic planning process
- ☐ Clear-cut executive commitment to perform a current state operational study - if not done prior to strategic planning
- ☐ Vertical, core competence or distributed operational capability
- ☐ Mergers and acquisitions
- ☐ Changes in product
- ☐ Outsource definitions
- ☐ Export plans
- ☐ Planned capacity expansions
- ☐ Programmable and/or computer controlled equipment
- ☐ Changes in the business model
- ☐ Significant operational changes
- ☐ Definition of requirements to build the smart enterprise
- ☐ Plans for automation and robotics

Critical decision

If there is no strategy by this point, call it quits and have a cold beer. The party is over – or should be.

Translatable Strategic Definitions

All strategy influences the information system. Translate strategies into sets of ERP functionality. Following are four examples.

Example 1 Strategy Statement: Mergers and Acquisitions

We will purchase at least one additional operation each year and integrate the information systems within six months of the acquisition.

Translation: the system must provide multi-plant and multi-company processing and the tools for easy integration. The chart of accounts will be a critical issue. The development of integration tools is required. The project team may be semi-permanent or permanent.

Example 2 Strategy Statement: Products

We will manufacture a product line offering customizable features using assemble to order concepts.

Translation: if the enterprise currently has a build to order or engineer to order fulfillment model, the information system must be able to support assemble to order. This is a major change affecting the information system, engineering, manufacturing, processes, and distribution.

Example 3 Strategy Statement: Procurement

We will outsource 50% of our purchased materials and components from China, India, Indonesia, and Mexico.

Translation: full supply chain functionality is required. The system must support multiple languages and currencies. While contemporary ERP systems incorporate full Internet processing, this requirement demands it. Companies engaged in supply chain programs also need lot size tracing and order tracking from the point of manufacture into their warehouse.

Example 4 Strategy Statement: Customer

We will immediately begin using supply chain collaboration as a tool for customer service and for future product development.

Translation: the system must support at least two levels of supply chain collaboration- information sharing and product development.

The information sharing functionality must be a part of the ERP system. Selected customers must be able to access information in the database regarding order and shipping status. This means real-time operations reporting. In addition, supply chain partners are collaborating in demand flow projects.

The requirement for product development may extend to electronic exchange of design criteria, color matching, engineering drawings, sharing bills of material and other relevant information. Product design frequently involves planning and coordinating activities.

A CRM solution appears to be a viable consideration covering all of these functions.

Strategy Requirements Stated for ERP Purposes

- ☐ Vertical, core competence and/or distributed operational capability
- ☐ Mergers and acquisitions
- ☐ Changes in product
- ☐ Definition of outsourcing plans
- ☐ Export plans
- ☐ Planned capacity expansions
- ☐ Changes to the business model
- ☐ Significant operational changes
- ☐ Two-page summary of strategies requiring computer-based information support (e.g. use of a business intelligence model)
- ☐ The business objective for this planning function is to synchronize the business systems to the various strategies
- ☐ There are frequently multiple business units, each with their own strategic and operational requirements that require integration
- ☐ Correlate these inputs to understand how the total system will work

Summary

If strategies cannot be stated in a two-page summary and approved by the President/CEO and the executive staff, stop the project before selecting the software. Selection is a matching process and strategies, are required to compare desire to capability.

Step 2 Current Operational State- Business Systems Assessment

Determining the Current Operational State is a high priority, extended, complex step. The process is both enlightening and disruptive. This formal business-planning activity logically follows the strategy definition. Its purpose is to evaluate the capability of the organization and its systems to execute the strategies. Although the system assessment may precede strategy development, it logically follows the establishment of high-quality strategic directions. These two steps, appropriately done, provide comprehensive inputs for developing the future business case.

The business needs assessment equates to a tactical and operational SWOT analysis.

1. Define strategies from Step 1 into software terms
2. Define tactical and operational capability
3. Match capability to strategic requirements
4. Evaluate and solve shortfall issues
5. Evaluate how to take advantage of opportunities
6. Define specific solutions in software terms

Because of its scope, ERP requires a comprehensive evaluation while specific purpose software often gets a more tailored approach. If, the goal is to install a Business Intelligence system, for example, and the enterprise systems are inaccurate or broken, there are benefits in performing a thorough assessment.

Business needs assessments are expensive and time-consuming but there are ways to manage the cost while accelerating the completion. They require using a structured process, Lean methodologies, working with vendors and consultants with integrity, providing the right priority, and focused training.

Internal Leadership

Permission to perform the assessment requires executive authorization from the president, chairperson of the board or other designee with the authority to get the job done right.

Traditionally, organizations assign ERP project responsibility to the financial and information technology departments. The most important leadership qualifications are the level of authority, working well in team environments, and business knowledge. Other consultants may downplay authority, but all projects have points requiring executive intervention. Even highly skilled project leaders will experience challenges to authority. Heading up a major systems study and project implementation is not a popularity contest nor is it a job for the fainthearted. Every business has secrets at all levels, but they must surface if they affect the business operations and need solutions defined in the future state.

Consultants

Consider hiring an experienced consultant for the assessment stage. They will be able to anticipate problems, view the enterprise through a different and practiced set of eyes, and get at the facts. Most consultants have highly structured approaches and programs, learned from leading or participating in multiple projects.

Consulting companies have established checklists used to focus and gain an in-depth assessment on the right issues. Lists provide useful and necessary insight about business processes and employees. Our checklists have nearly a thousand questions structured to determine how a process works plus its relationship to other processes.

A systematic shop floor tour will provide numerous answers, while generating additional questions.

If using a consulting firm establish the ground rules.

- ☐ Qualifications
- ☐ Affiliations
- ☐ Project scope
- ☐ Sequential vs. interactive project approach
- ☐ Schedules
- ☐ Accurate and precise billing process and inclusions
- ☐ Deliverables

Responsibilities

- ☐ Executive sponsor
- ☐ Executed by end associates
- ☐ Outside consultants

Objectives of the Study

- ☐ Study of business and information flow
- ☐ Internal leadership
- ☐ State of training
- ☐ Strength of systems
- ☐ Ability of the enterprise to achieve the strategies
- ☐ Define opportunities to improve the business

Metrics

- ☐ Establish metrics, both temporary and permanent
- ☐ Key performance indicators for this step
- ☐ Assign tasks and responsibilities

☐ Enforce responsibilities

Organize the Project

- ☐ Set up teams
- ☐ Provide strategic guidance
- ☐ Put together an assessment project plan
- ☐ Determine who will do the process mapping and how will it be accomplished
  - o Manually
  - o Business process mapping software
  - o Team/group
  - o Analyst
- ☐ Prepare a list of the documents to be gathered
- ☐ Establish dates for completion
- ☐ Establish how to compose the work teams
- ☐ Assign interviewee
- ☐ Set up the intensive planning sessions

Establish and Communicate the Project Philosophy

There are optional ways to organize the system study, covered in section one. They reappear here because this section stands alone as a check-off list. All the techniques apply in the appropriate environment.

Management needs cohesion on how to approach and accomplish the project. Following are two approaches, each very different. Keep in mind, the purpose is not generating a massive book to collect dust on a shelf, but investment in an actionable business plan.

Sequential (traditional)

- ☐ Questionnaires with 1000 questions resulting in three inch studies
- ☐ Credit goes to consultant or team performing the study who get their information from the workers

Interactive

- ☐ The thousand questions will get answered interactively
- ☐ Team flowcharting
- ☐ Team Intensive Planning (brainstorming) sessions at multiple levels
  - ☐ Executive, if possible, otherwise interview
  - ☐ Management
- ☐ User or process owner
  - ☐ General tools
  - ☐ Interviews
  - ☐ Surveys
  - ☐ Research (e.g.-comparative external data)
  - ☐ Process (value stream) mapping
  - ☐ Flowcharting
  - ☐ Photography
  - ☐ Video
- ☐ Credit goes to everyone for their inputs and cooperation

The method we at Affinity Systems recommend, fully support, and always use is the interactive process. We firmly believe that associates deserve credit for their contributions, and the report reflects their knowledge of the business. Additionally, and more importantly, if the reports are comprised of their recommendations, taking responsibility for making the solutions a reality as an extension of their thought processes and passions.

Inform the Organization

If the team approach is used, most employees will be involved in some form. It is important to enlist their aid.

Some form of communication outlining the project, the scope, the reason, and the objective is helpful. Failure to achieve buy in is an obstacle. Misrepresentation or lying will exacerbate the problem.

Train team members on assessment tools

Conduct assessments at the appropriate level of granularity. A high-level assessment can do the job for software vs. VMP options. Establishing and executing a complex project requires fine granularity and high-quality documentation of all processes.

The tools used for systems assessments have equal application in VMP.

- ☐ Process charts/Volume analysis
- ☐ User needs surveys and analysis
- ☐ Systems shortfalls
- ☐ Functionality needs list
- ☐ Functionality wants list
- ☐ Systems opportunities
- ☐ Capability analysis of current equipment to perform job
- ☐ Capability analysis of current staff
- ☐ Interfaces with customers / suppliers
- ☐ Operational constraints

Value Stream Mapping or Flow Charting

- ☐ What is the process
- ☐ Why is it done
- ☐ How is it done
- ☐ Who is doing it
- ☐ How long does it take
- ☐ Where is it being done
- ☐ What are the linkages
- ☐ Material flows

Do the work – major areas of focus

The intent of the study is to create a body of company knowledge: what, why and how it performs work, obtaining actionable information on how to change the business. If strategic planning precedes the study, it can focus on how well the current capabilities of the enterprise support those strategies instead of operational limitations.

Following is a partial process outline.

Functionality Assessment

The outcome of the exercise is to analyze the business as a process, providing executive management with actionable information.

The worst thing is for employees to withhold information on how they do their job and what problems or issues they encounter. The associates have significant knowledge about what works or is broken. Rooting out these systems and productivity problems, issues and concerns, are precisely the reasons for doing the assessment.

Need to address non-solution issues such as:

- Document the peak business cycle
- Actions to keep the business running
- Business metrics
- Manpower to maintain
- Financial requirements
- Organizational responsibilities
- Stockholder expectations
- Financial reports
- Surveys

Following are some of the areas of focus:

- Understanding the business
  - Current business processes
  - Operations
  - Office, not just operations
  - Branch locations where integration is either a given or a possibility

38

- Distribution

- Customer requirements and expectations
  - Level of customer satisfaction
  - Service metrics
  - Order fulfillment metrics
  - Ability to meet compliance specifications
  - Available to promise functionality
  - Order tracking, incoming and outgoing
  - On-line ordering capability

- Legal
  - Sarbanes-Oxley
  - Other regulatory compliance such as OSHA, EPA
  - Specialty materials permits
  - Intellectual property rights (contracts with consultants and software security provisions)
  - HR regulations

- Packaging requirements
  - Unique organizational requirements
  - RFID
  - Bar code
  - Special packaging requirements - internal
  - Special packaging requirements - customer

- Record accuracy
  - Bills of Material
  - Routings
  - Price
  - Cost
  - Inventory
  - Billing
  - Shipments
  - All Master Files

Two Examples – areas of focus

1. Customer service

- ☐ Determine accuracy of "Available to Promise"
- ☐ Document the order fulfillment process
- ☐ Document delivery performance - units ordered to units shipped
- ☐ Document delivery performance on complete orders
- ☐ Document the lead-time to customers on critical products
- ☐ Work all process flows through the office, shop and shipping

2. Inventory management

- ☐ Process map all systems and processes
- ☐ Document the replenishment times from suppliers through production to customer
- ☐ Document the number of manual transactions
- ☐ Calculate the rate of inventory turnover
  - ☐ Domestically produced by the enterprise
  - ☐ International
  - ☐ In transit export
- ☐ Sourced from international
- ☐ Shipping errors
- ☐ Ratio of right product to wrong product in stock
- ☐ Shrinkage in inventory
- ☐ Level of stock outs
- ☐ Level of expediting
- ☐ Analyze amount of write off at the end of year
- ☐ Determine need for annual physical inventory
- ☐ Receiving put away picking and shipping errors
- ☐ The accuracy of information on future receipts
- ☐ Does the location system accommodate - lot, containers, skids, part numbers, batch in relationship to rack, shelf, location

Methods

Use the principles of the scientific method. Enterprises involved in Lean are normally already familiar with these methods.

- [ ] Use functional teams
- [ ] Interview executive and key management personnel
- [ ] Define the 20-30 top Core business processes
- [ ] Review metrics and create new ones where they are needed
- [ ] Define enterprise (soul) uniqueness
- [ ] Build a series of lead-time and cycle-time charts to time phase the critical business cycles.
- [ ] Use process maps (by any name, e.g. Value Stream Mapping)) to document systems and processes.
- [ ] Pareto diagrams
- [ ] Affinity Charts
- [ ] Ask why, why, why then look past the answers to separate symptoms from problems

Assessment of Current Business Systems Functionality

- [ ] Volume analysis
- [ ] Transaction analysis and volume by type
- [ ] User needs analysis
- [ ] Systems shortfalls
- [ ] Systems opportunities
- [ ] Capability of current systems
- [ ] Document constraints
- [ ] Capability of current staff
- [ ] Interfaces with customers (e.g. collaboration programs, JIT programs)
- [ ] Interfaces with suppliers
- [ ] Define specific departmental needs
- [ ] Support of the business strategies
- [ ] Management of costs
- [ ] Study education needs of end associates

- ☐ Find the best solutions:
    - ☐ Formal systems
    - ☐ Informal systems
- ☐ Corporate culture
    - ☐ Unions
    - ☐ Existing paradigms
    - ☐ Management
        - ☐ Management style
        - ☐ Agendas

Assessment of Current ERP System Functionality

- ☐ Are there are hot lists on the shop floor?
- ☐ Are orders promptly processed?
- ☐ Do the workers trust the prints, process, and paperwork?
- ☐ Can you build a quality product using only formal, documented processes?
- ☐ Are the schedules executable?
- ☐ Are the reporting methods reliable and simple?
- ☐ Are the cutoffs logical?
- ☐ How many people are expediting materials?
- ☐ Are feeder departments on time with parts and components?
- ☐ Does the final assembly schedule freeze long enough to retain accuracy or it a moving target?
- ☐ Is the system fast enough to support information at the speed of reality?
- ☐ Does it incorporate mobile technology or integrate with available applications?
- ☐ Are ERP and Supply Chain systems integrated?

Information Systems Assessment

- ☐ Software Applications
    - ☐ ERP
    - ☐ SCM
    - ☐ MES

- ☐ Engineering
- ☐ Program quality

- ☐ Files and structures
  - ☐ Languages
  - ☐ Inventory by user (P.C.)
  - ☐ Identify associates by system
  - ☐ Upgrades
  - ☐ Licenses

- ☐ Authorized or unauthorized
  - ☐ Security applications
  - ☐ Reports and other user complied status data

- ☐ Document the extent to which the ERP system is used
  - ☐ Hardware
  - ☐ Inventory of equipment
  - ☐ Age
  - ☐ Capability
  - ☐ Upgrades/ Updates
  - ☐ Facility
  - ☐ Air conditioning
  - ☐ Mainframe
  - ☐ Distributed

- ☐ Remote support requirements

- ☐ Document ERP modules currently used
  - ☐ Sales Forecasting
  - ☐ Customer Order Processing
  - ☐ Engineering Data Control
  - ☐ Inventory Control
  - ☐ Master Scheduling
  - ☐ Material Requirements Planning
  - ☐ Purchasing
  - ☐ Sales and Operations Planning

- ☐ Capacity Planning
- ☐ Operation Scheduling
- ☐ Shop Floor Control
- ☐ Customer Relationship Management (CRM) – Marketing automation
- ☐ Sales Force Automation – (SFA) Customer support
- ☐ Product Lifecycle Management (PLM)
- ☐ Product Data Management (PDM)
- ☐ Supply Chain Management (SCM)
- ☐ Warehouse management System
- ☐ Inventory management
- ☐ Supply Chain collaboration (SCC)
- ☐ Field Service
- ☐ Financial Planning and Budgeting
- ☐ Manufacturing Execution Systems (MES)
- ☐ Tooling files
- ☐ Content Management System
- ☐ Document Management Systems
- ☐ Quality Management Systems
- ☐ Asset Management Systems
- ☐ Multi-Plant processing
- ☐ Governance
- ☐ Intelligence Applications
- ☐ Energy Management
- ☐ Mobile technology

- ☐ Integration with other systems
  - ☐ Internet
  - ☐ Telephone
  - ☐ Fax
  - ☐ EDI
  - ☐ Machine tools
  - ☐ Support tools
  - ☐ Mobile devices
  - ☐ Robots

- ☐ Key metrics currently used

- ☐ Client server vs. mainframe
  - ☐ Number of associates
  - ☐ State of the database
  - ☐ Functionality of the programs and the hardware
  - ☐ Data collection

- ☐ Data
  - ☐ Test record accuracy – office and operations
  - ☐ Gather samples of all documents and define precisely how they are used
  - ☐ Gather transaction volumes
  - ☐ Record accuracy – test counts paperwork and real world use
  - ☐ Test record accuracy including B/M, inventory, routings, etc.

Systems to be included in the study

- ☐ Accounting and Finance
- ☐ Marketing Information
- ☐ Human Resource systems
- ☐ Administrative functions
- ☐ Sales and Customer Service
- ☐ Order Processing / allocation
- ☐ Master scheduling
- ☐ Engineering
- ☐ Products – lifecycle management (PLM), new product development
- ☐ Inventory management
- ☐ Manufacturing
- ☐ Warehousing
- ☐ Distribution
- ☐ Supply Chain
- ☐ Business Intelligence

- ☐   Customer Relationship Management
- ☐   Purchasing
- ☐   Forecasting
- ☐   Inbound logistics
- ☐   Supplier relationship management/collaboration
- ☐   Transportation – outbound logistics

Analyze the data

This analysis determines if the current system is capable of achieving strategies and the operational requirements. Compile the results for executive management.

- ☐ External pressures
- ☐ Internal pressures
  - ☐ Executive direction
- ☐ Information systems relationships
  - ☐ Cause and effect to other systems
  - ☐ Strategy definition
  - ☐ Interviews
  - ☐ Intensive planning sessions

There will be contradictory information. Many issues stated as problems are symptoms. Pursue each issue until the root cause is exposed. Remove emotion from the process. Support all conclusions with data.

Team recommendations

The second part of the report includes team recommendations to executive management, who must authorize/participate in the future state development. The report may indicate how much trouble the company is in and the cost of correction.

Include problem statements, metrics, survey results, interviews, and questionnaires in the analysis.

There will be political pressures by some to exclude unfavorable information. Those persons preparing the document must not participate in a cover-up for several reasons. First, it is a matter of personal integrity. Second, executive management cannot fix unknown situations. Third, when the truth emerges, the least consequence will be ruined reputations.

Make sure the executive staff gets the whole picture.

If the pressure becomes too great, or the authority level is high, submit an individual confidential report to the Executive Champion and President/CEO.

The consultant can play an important role in getting critical data to the right place. He/she is not concerned with internal politics or hiding information, nor do they have to live with offended persons after the project is completed. In addition, we view it as part of our job to make sure executive management has accurate and complete facts. If there is controversy in this area, let us take one for the team.

Analysis

- ☐ Build optimal solutions
- ☐ Support the broad needs of the business – build in adaptability
- ☐ Improve the customer service systems
    - ☐ Speed of production
    - ☐ Speed of information
    - ☐ Product quality
    - ☐ Timeliness
    - ☐ Customer relationships
- ☐ Management of costs
    - ☐ Smart, fast operational systems
    - ☐ Productivity improvement base
        |
- ☐ Find the best solutions
    - ☐ Formal systems
    - ☐ Informal systems

- ☐ Resolve non-ERP issues
  - ☐ Workers to maintain security and data integrity
  - ☐ Workers to support day-to-day operations
  - ☐ Remote support requirements

Summary

The inability of business processes to support the strategies and operations of the business indicate the system is broken in some way. Some ERP systems are not, nor were ever capable of supporting the business requirements. There are only two choices, live with it or replace it.

Step 3 Planned Future State - Conceptual Plan

The future state is the business blueprint, defining each systems component, how it will function, interact, and perform work. It is a layered, modular assessment forming the core for all subordinate plans, including the project plan. Properly done, it cascades from strategy through ERP selection criteria, serving as a foundation for continuous improvement processes, both evolutionary and transformative.

The future state has many labels, including conceptual plan, future vision, and business process modeling. Look past the labels and focus on the principles.

While there are economic arguments against the future state, it is remarkable given the 40-year history of ERP systems that numerous projects move into implementation without one. Some companies think it is a non-value added activity. Others view it as a cost avoidance opportunity. Regardless of the reason, bypassing the step is a false economy.

Speed

Business activities are an effect of the marketplace and competitive pressures, changing the strategies and information requirements. The increase in business necessitates rapid information assimilation.

Software converts data into information. Information systems are strategic and therefore, software belongs to management. Fast, high-volume information flows fuel the smart enterprise.

Business is under extreme pressure to perform faster while supplying a rapid succession of personalized new products. This translates into smaller run quantities with shorter demand horizons and order to cash processes. Output continues towards the theoretical goal of one to one production. Customers' experiences need to be positive, whether it is buying home furnishings or a new car. In the new instant world, online reviews punish poor product or service performance.

Automation

Automation has dramatically collapsed production cycle times, altering the way information is captured and used. Contemporary systems drive manufacturing machines directly from designs. Automation, including event reporting and sensors, collect data from the shop floor, warehouse, transportation, and supply chain. Real-time data capture dramatically increases the volume of data to organize, store, and process. Database systems need to be integrated, powerful, scalable, and capable of converting large data volumes into usable information. Automation speeds up both the operational and information reality.

Computing Power and Data Transmission Speeds

Businesses were once concerned with the high cost and availability of storage and processing. Computer programs and methods considered these factors. One example is batch processing. Computers were not fast or large enough to support real-time transaction processing at every level, lacking the ability to provide users with a continuous stream of information.

These limitations have disappeared. Now users have a choice about when/how to use batch, real-time or a combination of techniques. Companies without storage capacity can purchase it at reasonable prices on the cloud. The rapid accumulation of relevant data, storage, and super-fast conversion into information is one of the keys to the smart enterprise.

E-Commerce

The second part of the computing power equation is bandwidth or Internet speed. Businesses and individuals can transmit large volumes of data/information anywhere in the world, and/or interact with business and each other in real-time.

The Internet provides alternatives to traditional on-premise information processing. While bundled under a cloud label, this is Software as a Service (SaaS), where processing takes place at a remote server. Rented software, priced on usage, replaces software normally purchased and installed on-premise.

Internet applications are propelling enterprises into ever-higher velocity opportunities with worldwide integration capabilities. This will enable transformation into virtual enterprises, with the option to bypass traditional plant integration.

Mobile Technology

Mobile technology has moved the information reality from the office to the world, from voice to image and text, from status to content rich streaming flows. Actionable information is real-time and social media such as Facebook and Linked-In enables global collaboration. The differences between hand-held devices and PCs are increasingly blurred, separated more by personal choice and ease of use than functionality. The technology as applied to business is equally pervasive. Orders are tracked from any location as the product moves through the factory, warehouse, and onto the truck. GPS follows the order location in transit, and notifies the customer the second it arrives.

Today, Mobile devices facilitate pricing, order inquiry, available to promise, placing orders, shop reporting, and order picking. This technology consumes data in enormous volumes, and significantly contributes to information at the speed of reality. ERP databases unable to support these devices are technically obsolete.

Big Data

Businesses are capturing large volumes of real-time data from multiple sources, including   enterprise, vendors, and customers. This creates a condition labeled "big data." Where prior evolutions of technology left business searching for viable analytical data, the current issue is how to manage and convert the data into useful information products.

The resolution of big data is critical. If you are performing due diligence for a new system, there is a high probability the business is not processing information at the speed of reality. If this becomes a critical selection criterion, then big data is in your future. Include the resolution in the future state and integration plans.

Analytics

Enterprises have embraced the use of "business intelligence" tools. These come in a variety of sizes and shapes from simple drill down to complex analytics. The objective is to have functionality that builds information products-visualization, decision support, sales analysis, etc. in a timely and trustworthy fashion. Some programs require setting up reporting point codes within the software.

Include analytics in the future state and integration plans. Analytics may not be available in some standard packages, but provide useful functionality. Operational priority dictates rock solid ERP tools. The lack of features available as third party applications cannot override the core requirements if the balance of the package is the best fit for your business.

A number of companies offer analytic software. Some are IBM, SAP, Oracle, Microsoft SharePoint, Epicor, SAP Crystal Reports, Alteryx, Pentaho, and GE Intelligent Platforms. Suppliers also offer analytics through the SaaS format. An excellent guide is available at http://www.pentaho.com/resources/pdf-stream/20/the-ultimate-guide-to-buying-business-analytics.

The Cloud

Cloud organizations rent storage and software services, paid for by subscription or amount of service used. The following illustration provides visual definition.

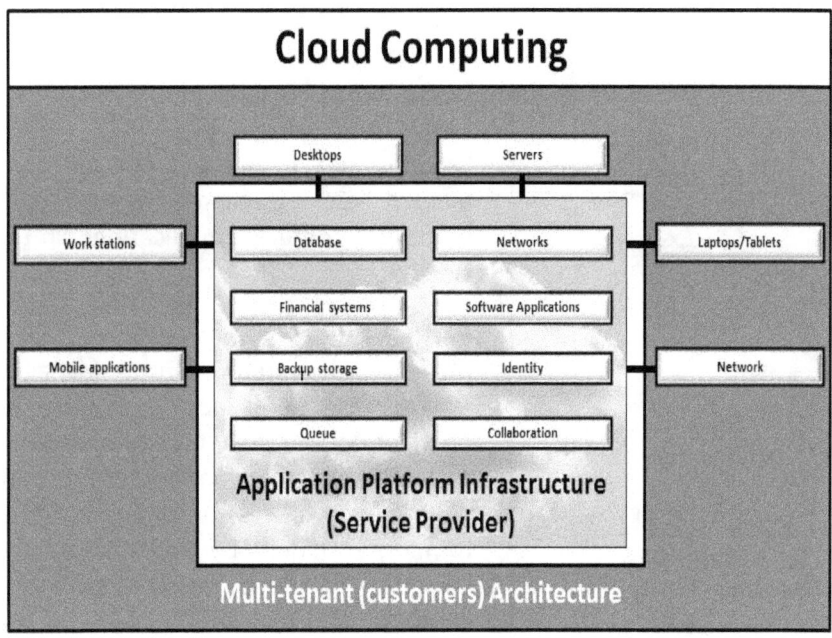

Illustration-Cloud

Application Service Provider

Synonymous with the growth of the World Wide Web, software companies developed downloadable products, including software used "as is," like virus protection and operating systems. Program development followed specific principles, protocols, and procedures. As Service-Oriented Architecture (SOA) evolved, Application Service Provider (ASP) replicated the old service bureaus, offering information-processing services using proprietary software.

The cloud involves processing multi-tenant customers on single or multiple offsite computers. Information may be stored anywhere in the cloud, without the customer knowing its specific location.

ASP is the new service bureau. The utility owns the software and has multiple customers using it. Computers transmit data from one digital device to another via high-speed networks. One or more devices reside in the on-premise system, and another is at the provider. Virtual systems allow nearly unlimited numbers of inquiries from computers or mobile devices.

| IT Staff |
| Development Staff |

| Operating System |
| E-Mail |
| Web presence |
| ERP System |
| Business Intelligences/ Analytics |
| Customer Relationship Management |
| Financial systems |
| HR |
| Data Collection |
| Backup |

| Web browsers |
| Work stations |
| Mainframe |
| Distributed |
| Networks |

Software as a Service (SaaS)

SaaS expands on all the above concepts, but is one method among many referencing different applications "in the cloud."

Gartner defines SaaS as "software that is owned, delivered, and managed remotely by one or more providers. The provider delivers an application based on a single set of common code and data definitions, which is consumed in a one-to-many model by all contracted customers anytime on a pay-for-use basis, or as a subscription based on use metrics."

The software applications reside on a provider's computer, on their site or through a network, providing different levels of services.

A traditional IT department, called "on-premise" in SaaS, has staff, hardware, operating systems, and software applications.

54

The next illustration shows the hierarchy of the services and their relationship in the cloud.

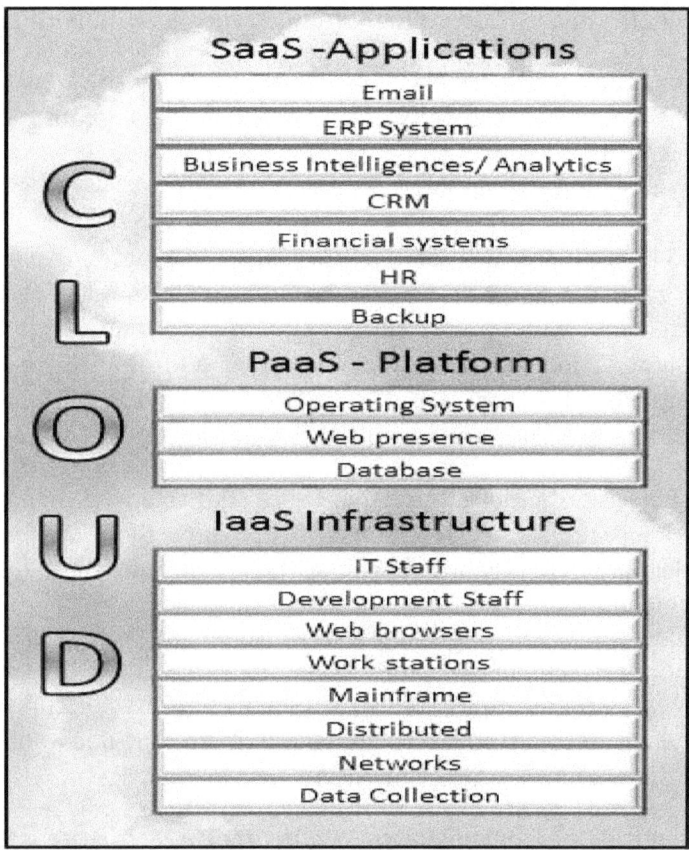

Illustration-SaaS Applications

For example, moving the analytics application blocks from on-premise to software provided by the supplier is SaaS if the service provider is multi-tenant.

A customer has the option of outsourcing all or part of their information needs, including ERP, with the exception of resources needed to capture and process data on-premise. Under the IaaS format, even these are candidates for outsourcing.

Infrastructure as a Service (IaaS) relates to the old facilities management concept. The service provider owns the equipment and is responsible for running and managing the applications. In effect, it moves the entire IT department from on-premise to service provider.

Platform as a Service (PaaS) addresses IT issues. The SaaS Company owns the servers and software. Your internally generated transactions are transmitted offsite and processed. Streaming information flows back to your organization.

SaaS applications, with off-site programs and processing over the web, are catching on with on-premise users. While relevant to smaller companies with non-complex ERP functionality, it has greater application for analytics, CRM, and other non-shop related functions. Some tier one and two ERP software suppliers have strategically committed to SaaS, and have products on the market.

SaaS decisions require the IT hardware staff to advise management on the implications of each option. The problem is the IT staff jobs may be in jeopardy. A reliable consulting firm will guide you through this evaluation.

There are various competitive fee structures, and it requires due diligence to understand them. SaaS either extends or complicates the software decision process - sometimes both, but does not become a factor until future state solutions are developed.

As with all new technologies, finding the right partner is the key to success. Some providers of on-demand software, not all ERP, are PLEX Online, Sage Peachtree, Visibility, NetSuite, Epicor Express, Aplicor, Intacci, and Sales Force.

The selection process leading up to the ERP decision is the same for cloud applications as on-premise. The cloud carries the potential for significant savings in staff and equipment. Executive management and auditors must address the issues of security, business continuity, and implement control protocols.

Integration

The ability to integrate systems seamlessly is partially dependent on the software type and its capability.

An integrated system offers full functionality to a vertical industry, such as manufacturing, distribution, or construction. Decomposing the manufacturing vertical one layer results in the following business types: process, repetitive, or engineer to order. The type of processes they use, for example, metal casting, fabrication, machining, and/or assembly further defines the business activity and required functionality.

General-purpose software addresses the core needs of a vertical, providing broader but less detailed functionality. Conversely, best of breed or industry-specific software more precisely addresses narrower but deeper requirements. Consequently, industry-specific software is normally less expensive and requires less modification during implementation.

The decomposition eventually stops at functionality, where there is a proliferation of software applications such as Customer Relationship Management (CRM), analytics, Manufacturing Execution Systems (MES), Point of Sales, literally every application imaginable. Like any software product, the quality and price varies across the bell curve

The downside is that functionality beyond the specialty, often purchased separately, requires integration. A fully integrated system incorporates the same protocols - language, files, and labels. That is clearly not always the reality.

Although the debate continues comparing best practices and integrated software, tools exist to integrate most systems. The issue is cost, time, and result. The problems are the differences in format, field sizes, formulas used, programming language, and database technology. Each system is dissimilar in size and calculation, and conversion is required to move data back and forth from one software product to the other. The reconciliation of these issues is basic to any form of automated integration, but the mashed result may prove that the sum total is worse than its parts.

Software code, defining how data is processed into useful information, is relatively static. Modifications can be complicated and expensive. The term flexible information system is an oxymoron in some poorly structured software. ERP is a set of tightly designed and written procedures for executing repetitive formulas, requiring designed-in flexibility.

Flexibility comes in four forms. The first is architecture, where designed and coded functionality provide a number of solution pathways through seamless modules. The second level of flexibility is the ability to modify systems codes, features and functions, and upload or download data, sometimes into custom written subroutines. User fields add flexibility but lack the integrated functionality of standard system fields. The third flexibility is plug and play functionality for integrating third party or best of breed software. Adding significant ERP functionality such as CRM or Supply Chain Management (SCM) results in a system labeled "Extended ERP." The forth form of flexibility is modularity/apps, providing the ability to match/snap application components together.

The decision to use industry specific or an integrated software package carries an implicit commitment to some level of integration, and for that reason, it is a critical selection criteria.

Companies Not Using an ERP System

The number of small companies skews the percentage using ERP. These companies, like contract manufacturers, may use engineering systems to drive production. Nearly all larger companies use ERP systems, but the smaller ones are finding help on the cloud. Using simple MRP systems is another option.

Companies with Obsolete Systems

Many companies are one or more software generations behind because they failed to apply upgrades. There are/were reasons for not updating on schedule. To avoid postponing the problem, resolve these issues before taking action. If the system is working correctly, logic dictates that upgrades would be a natural part of the process. If delays occurred because a major reimplementation is involved, weigh the value of staying with the current software and performing the upgrade, or buying and implementing a new ERP system.

Current systems may be working correctly, but lack the functionality to deal with the new rules of speed and technology, or the business has outgrown its capabilities. The solution is to acquire a system providing the required solutions.

Manufacturing and Distribution

Those familiar with manufacturing often believe distribution functions, including warehouse management systems (WMS) and shipping functionality, are extensions of any ERP system. Some manufacturing consultants think distribution has fewer complex processes. Both perspectives are incorrect. Distributors have intricate picking and fulfillment processes, including subassemblies, packaging, and conversion of product from one form to another. We recommend that companies with complex manufacturing and distribution requirements understand these differences, and acquire software specifically addressing these multiple and sometimes conflicting conditions.

Software Sophistication

Software suppliers service each market niche. Many of the features overlap, but the functionality varies widely in quality and scope. This diversity of both product and suppliers make software selection tedious and difficult. Companies must make the commitment to do the work or risk being stuck with mismatched or unsupported ERP systems.

Many software companies have rewritten their packages with all applications and functionality in the same language, on common databases. These systems are truly integrated with every module working in sync by design, instead of being mashed together using real or conceptual middleware. Ask each software company how the system is constructed. If it is a mashed system, give it a negative weighting.

Environmental Scanning - Results

- [ ] Establish the current and future business states.
- [ ] Is the business model still correct?
- [ ] What is the driving force? Exercise great caution in defining and changing the driving force. We recommend acquiring a copy of "Top Management Strategy, What it is, and How to Make It Work', written by Benjamin B. Tregoe and John W. Zimmerman.
- [ ] If not what is the new model?
- [ ] Review the mission – is it still the target for directing asset utilization and marketing efforts?
- [ ] Is the enterprise agile (able to react quickly), Lean (efficient) and adaptive (intelligent, proactive and change oriented)?

Mapping Future to Current States

The future state plan maps the business capabilities, determined by the need's assessment, to the business strategies. It identifies gaps between the two and provides actionable solutions to achieve the strategies.

The future state map is a transitional conceptualization of the system components, per the series of illustrations developed with various clients. We have found that putting the plan in a visual form helps understand and document the process. An actual future state is complex with greater granularity than the ones shown. Each of these illustrations communicates the design and its implications throughout the organization.

The plan should contain layers of detail on how the system works and how the design supports the objectives. The intent is to document the current state per the above activities, and construct the future state, including the top 30 business applications by developing business case scenarios and process designs. When completed, everyone will have a far more comprehensive understanding of how the business works and the changes required to achieve both long and short-term goals.

Map of the Future State
Process Designs

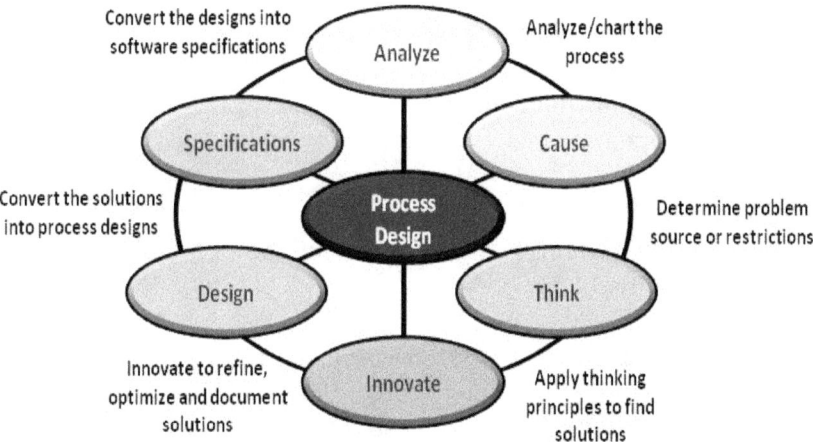

The steps are similar to those presented for the ACTION VMP methodology covered in Step 9.

1. Analyze - analyze and chart the process.
2. Cause - Determine problem or source of constraints/restrictions
3. Think - Apply the thinking principles to find solutions
4. Innovate - Refine, optimize, and document solutions
5. Design - Convert the solutions into process designs
6. Specifications - Convert the designs into software specifications

Business redesigns frequently are developed and implemented through a series of iterations per the following business operation systems.

ERP System

The chart on the next page shows an integrated layout for a manufacturing company. It superimposes the core closed loop system over an operational structure, and then expands it with contemporary functionality, all wrapped inside of a real-time processing environment.

- ☐ Multi-plant processing
- ☐ Analytics
- ☐ CRM
- ☐ Supply chain management
- ☐ MES
- ☐ Customer distribution system
- ☐ Collaboration
- ☐ Energy

The Distribution system version appears in the appropriate location later in this chapter.

Regardless of your business type, specific key processes exist within the functional enterprise. A larger copy, titled ERP Lessons Learned Illustrations PDF, contains the illustrations from this book, and charts for health care, construction, agri-business, and distributors. It is downloadable from CompetitiveAmerica.us.

The ERP system shown is for a highly advanced manufacturing company incorporating all the potential functions. Some of the differences are the use of an MES to replace the normal shop floor (PAC) module, CRM, analytics and energy planning.

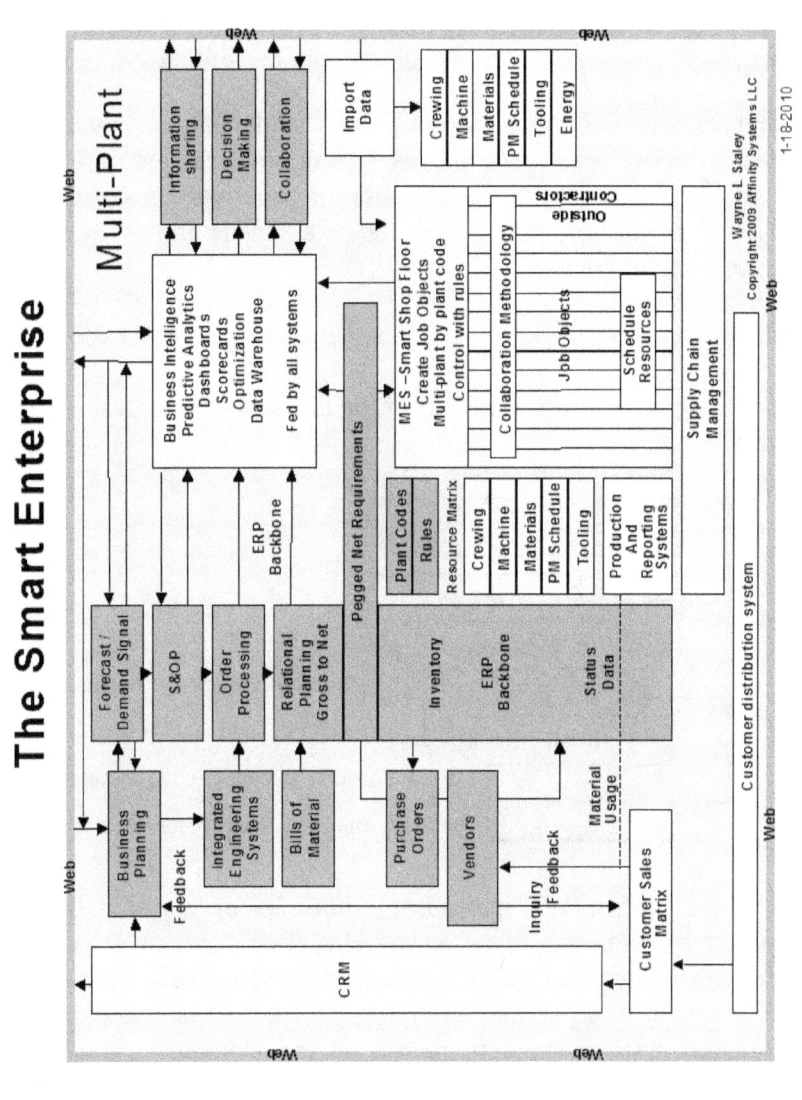

Illustration - The Smart Enterprise

63

Work through this chart and determine needed information systems functionality for your business. If any of these labels is unfamiliar, "ERP Information at the Speed of Reality," provides definitions, but an Internet search on the labels will provide summary knowledge.

An Implicit element within the designs is the elimination of paperwork, replaced with real-time images. Computers/Tablets are within everyone's budget, and the elimination of paperwork provides a rapid dollar and environmental payback. Define a backup process in case of a massive systems failure.

Engineering

Engineering systems are the heart of the ERP system and deserve a high priority.

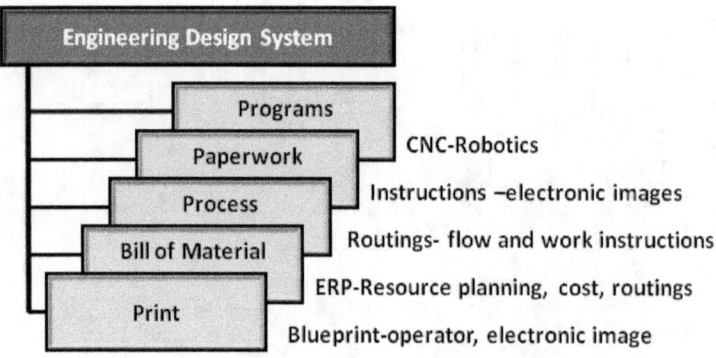

ERP starts with prints, processes, and bills of material, normally managed and maintained by engineering. Our experience has shown that many companies go into the selection process without a full understanding of what they are getting into. Companies with heavily engineered systems need to review all the elements paying special attention to relationships and data integrity. The success of ERP lies in the integrity of the engineering system, starting with accurate database information, derived from properly structured bills of material and routings. ERP software addresses a complex set of program options and engineering requirements. Many engineering departments use third party systems such as Finite-Element Analysis and Solid Modeling, which directly or indirectly interface with the ERP system.

ERP systems must integrate design engineering and automated production systems. Modern production equipment blurs the dividing line between data needed for ERP, engineering and the shop. Production machines run directly from computer designs without the use of ERP and are computers themselves.

Companies with complex BOM must extend relational planning far into the engineering and manufacturing processes. Conversely, companies with fewer complexities, like distribution, may not need sophisticated engineering functionality, yet require kitting functionality.

Modular Designs

Modular design structurally breaks a product down into smaller parts or components. Each part is replicable, interchangeable, and scalable. The method supports mass production and mass customization, depending on the level of design granularity.

Modular design capability is a core principle within repetitive ERP systems supporting manufacturing, and supply chain flexibility. The breakdown of bill of material (BOM) in Engineer to Order companies also follows the principle, with the majority of parts designed for interchangeability because of service requirements. The design starts at the finished product, then subassemblies, parts, and raw materials.

Modular design facilitates configuring products, allowing customers to select from a list of options. Anyone who has purchased merchandise over the Internet is familiar with the concept. An example is clothing. The first menu provides an option for style. Selecting the style brings up a size menu. Selecting the size brings up color. Selecting this last option, the buyer takes the order to the checkout.

Modular designs provide flexibility. Users thoroughly understand the bill of material and structure. The process enables flattening the number of tiers by adding routing data, thereby reducing inventory and speeding up production.

Modular design makes it simpler to split production of components or finished product from multiple producers. It works for SCM, supporting modifications in the distribution center.

Product Design Responsibility

Product design is not the sole providence of engineering. In some business models such as distribution, responsibility belongs to marketing and sales. Frequently, they do not require sophisticated engineering software but need system's functionality for color match, and multiple language conversion.

Legacy Systems

Companies with legacy systems will know how to convert engineering data to the new ERP system, but must take the time to review and rationalize the entire engineering process. Factor the effect of visual or Lean methodologies and expanded shop floor control applications into the review.

Companies installing their first ERP systems will struggle with BOM structuring. Numbering systems will be a specific problem. Be prepared to spend an inordinate amount of time on these activities but have patience. It is critical to get them right.

Same as except

Sample production is a game-changing application. The first prototype to the customer often determines who gets the business. This places extreme pressure on engineering and manufacturing, and there is frequently little time to prepare a new BOM. The software must support "same as except" with the online ease of crossing off one part number and writing in another.

It must be easy to enter designs into the database. This is a complaint that ETO's and contractors have with iterative ERP systems. For them, the bill is the equivalent of the gross level production schedule, and maintaining the BOM may be a redundant effort. With high levels of ECN (engineering change notices), it can be a non-value adding activity for engineering and production, but other departments and functions need the information, such as purchasing and finance.

Rapid quote entry provides tracking and facilitates conversion into orders.

Lead-time Offsets

ERP manages time by using lead-time offsets. The three most-used factors are:

1. The bill of material planning horizon
2. Cycle time is comprised of queue, move, and run times, defining the length of time required, given the available resources, from the start to the completion of the product as planned. Machine, and process time all share the "cycle time" label.
3. From a customer's perspective, lead-time is the elapsed time from order entry until the product arrives on the dock.

Specifying the right offsets is important. Plans with excessive offset time results in surplus work in process and capacity used prior to need. Specifying unrealistically short offsets understates the process time, resulting in production planned to be late.

Calculated lead-times separate tiers, reflecting the total queue, (run, and move sequence), used to time phase production.

Summing all lead-times from each level equals the theoretical product cycle time. The due dates for each part are calculated and used for the shop schedules.

Time offsets are required, even if minimal. They calculate product completion dates, the capacity plan and synchronize output. In a

Kanban application, the supplier must still be able to replenish or fill demand in a timely fashion.

Nearly all ERP systems calculate and maintain the lead-time onsets. This does not mean abdication of responsibility to monitor and manage the system. The prudent act is to set up a periodic review schedule and audit the system.

Routings and Work Centers

Routings are a list of actions and work center operations required to make a part, component, sub-assembly, or final product. Routings, or operation sequences, are determined by engineering or manufacturing engineering. They contain the cost and time elements from work centers, and used to plan capacity, labor, tooling, and crewing requirements. The standard cost system includes material, labor and burden or material, labor, burden and variable burden.

Requirements planning systems calculate and time phase customer requirements, inventories, materials, labor, machines, tooling, and paperwork. Workflow and operational planning use routings attached to the part numbers. Routings and work centers plan asset utilization and manage cost information.

Companies using average cost systems need to guarantee that ERP software candidates support the methodology. Some packages advertise average cost solutions, but make sure the supplier demos this functionality to the complete satisfaction of your accountants and auditors.

Use routing records and bills of material to build up costs through the production chain, from raw materials through finished goods. Routing accuracy has financial implications.

Tooling

This is a database of jigs, fixtures, cutting tools and other equipment required by a process, for a setup or specific part production. Tooling is part of routing and work center information.

Group Technology

There are additional options on the BOM. Group technology (GT) codes break product into finite, geometric shapes, functions, and characteristics. Group technology codes are descriptive, sortable, and highly significant. Engineering owns this field. It is a logical number for accessing a database in engineering terms and it maintains the significant data washed out of the item or part number. It is easier to group parts into families, control databases and to manage prints.

Configuration, Features and Options

The features and option's functionality may be as useful for the ETO as for other business types. If required, make sure they are native to the package. Configuration management falls in this same category. Identify these types of requirements in the need's assessment. This is one reason to get professional help in evaluating your system requirements.

Abundant information on configuration management, features, and options is available, and companies need to do the research. With the widespread use of the web, these are valuable tools. The additional design and color match tools are generally not part of an ERP system. Many companies use Macs for design purposes. It is important to dig deeply and understand how all the options interact, and what software tools you need to get the job done right.

Production and Engineering Systems

ERP requires multiple transactions reporting points throughout the production and inventory chain, including production, receiving, and disbursal. (See the closed-loop ERP system illustration on page 10).

Engineering Change

The need for complex engineering change management varies by business. Some manufacturers need comprehensive ECN procedures. All companies need version control for maintenance, quality, and troubleshooting purposes. Drug companies are one example. They have to control the product from the cradle to grave. Product liability avoidance demands proper record keeping.

Pegged Requirements

Pegging is a process populating the independent demand SKU into all requirements' records, and frequently the customer order number. Full level pegging is carrying the order number and/or SKU through every requirement and order record. This provides the ability to trace parts, shop or purchase orders back to specific customer orders.

ERP companies supply a variety of pegging logic, so make sure the method supplied by the software candidate meets your needs. Due diligence requires companies to evaluate how they want to manage, track orders and parts related to a specific order, finished product, parts or materials.

Pegging enables reporting by the order number for tracking purposes, and for capturing actual cost information. Heavily engineered complex product manufacturers need full level pegged requirements capability. Pegging provides "where used" by product, order number, or specific parts. BTOs also use pegged records for capturing actual cost data.

Some systems carry the order number down only one level. This is sufficient where components and parts appear on summarized work orders and order pegging synchronizes parts into the final assembly schedule.

Database

The database contains the master records and transactions. The original database (DB) concept is that all records of the business reside in one location. This prevented having to maintain the same data in multiple locations, a redundant and unnecessary requirement. Today, the database concept is more sophisticated and allows data to be broken into smaller chunks, and logical records may reside in many physical locations, or somewhere on the cloud.

The purpose, however, is still to provide a common data source to the user community, made more urgent by the proliferation of mobile technology and its insatiable appetite for information. Everyone contributes to and enriches the data pool. Regardless of data standardization, the information obtained may be different when multiple programs use the same information but dissimilar calculations.

Most of the SaaS providers integrate mobile technologies, but the issue is - do they integrate with, or replace, potential on premise databases?

Database Update Timing

Batch processing describes accumulating transactions throughout the day and processing the ERP calculations and updates on a predefined schedule, normally overnight. Batch processing includes master file changes and all operational transactions.

Real time means updating and processing transactions as they occur. Early computers did not have the power or speed to achieve real time processing. The restriction today is cost, not capability.

If companies want to take advantage of sophisticated BI or drastically speed up business agility, ERP systems must provide information at the speed of reality. This integration is both strategic and operational. Think about it now, not after the money is committed. Speed of decision-making depends on the software system, but fast information is of lesser value when the physical operation is constrained and the business unable to react. A specific plan, including ERP and Lean Six

Sigma principles is ideal for building high-velocity production and distribution systems.

As stated earlier, many installations use a blend of batch and real-time processing in balance.

Master Files

There are dozens of individual files, which collectively comprise the database. The major files are the item master, customer master, and vendor master, bills of material (product structure), routings, and work centers.

The Master Item File contains specific information about product, components, parts, and materials. This includes design and related specification's data to the Item Master and Bill of Material (Product Structure) files. It states ordering, inventory rules for each item, and maintains status data such as inventory balances. To this list, add chaining to shop information, routings and work center information, maintained by engineering or manufacturing. The item file, and how it is structured, will play a significant role in the success of your installation.

The history of ERP implementations is replete with examples of the importance and complexity of dealing with the Master item file. It is one of the main sources for extending implementations. Everyone owns a portion, and it affects the entire organization. Marketing manages the finished product, manufacturing controls the routing, and engineering owns the model number. It is not enough to tell the team to "get it done." Executive Management must delegate ownership of the master file conversion to a specific team of marketing, sales, engineering, and manufacturing personnel with direction from IT.

The coding and classification structures behind these files are important and demand attention, but the plant code illustrates the effect on the selection process.

Plant Codes

When every file and record contains plant codes, the systems are multi-plant or multi-company. This means that a number of plants with autonomous databases can use one system. Each can operate with its own chart of accounts, yet roll up all data for corporate wide planning purposes. All the information is selectively available for the facilities by design, instead of compiled from mixed files and reports.

If the system lacks multi-plant capability, it often uses different codes to split up information, making it appear like multi-plant. In these cases, there can normally be only one chart of accounts. The records for multiple locations are stored on one set of files, where anyone using the system has access to data from other facilities. Ask your software company for a detail breakdown of all files and fields and check if codes apply to all modules. Your system may require planning production and transfer of material between disparate locations, and multiple plant functionalities is required to accomplish this goal.

Part Numbers

The part, product, or model number is normally the stock keeping unit or SKU. The packaging demands of the mega-merchandisers can place extraordinary pressure on finding a way to call different packaging configurations the same number. An example is an eight pack for one customer and a six-pack for others. While there are schemes or work around, they will cause confusion, excessive cost, and lack of control. Bear in mind, there can be only one SKU per discrete part number.

There has been a long-running debate about part numbers. Should they be significant, carrying descriptive information or non-significant, that is, purely numeric. Internationalism supports this approach. So does internet processing with menus or configurations. This debate is not as simple as it appears although both often contain data, such as size. Engineering, production, inventory personnel, and sales all use short descriptive numbers. Computers can use either method. Current convention favors the non-significant part number or minimal alphanumeric data.

Each company must resolve the numbering system issue, but one word of caution. Trying to change numbering systems while selecting and installing an ERP system is dangerous. It introduces complex variables on top of other significant variables. Item numbers are meaningful, determined, and controlled by engineering. IT and engineering normally have the best perception of the usage and the price to change them. Modifying SKU formats automatically requires changes to history, orders, inventory, locations, bar codes, and customer records. Think about how the number will affect forecasts, demand driven systems, customer, vendor ERP systems, and internal control mechanisms.

Make sure the system can accommodate your number. Never modify a part number field on the software programs. It is the record key and permeates the entire system. A change to the field size is a major programming task. Either the field is big enough and usable, or it is not. Never compromise on this issue with a supplier. Find the right package.

Descriptions

The description is an alphanumeric field used to put meaningful information into useful sequences. Most shop associates have these numbers memorized and use them constantly. Any analysis of part numbers will include descriptions. If a non-significant part number is used, the description becomes more meaningful. Descriptions often have variable formats, making it difficult to sort into useful sequences. Check how the system uses helper fields, such as commodity codes or user fields. They are set up like system's codes and established early in the implementation process.

Product Categories

Product codes and classifications differentiate product types. Product categories are summarized part numbers and descriptions. These occur within different parts of the system, primarily sales and materials. The sales department uses the code to differentiate types of sales and marketing activities. Purchasing summarizes materials by category to analyze cost, usage, and purchasing patterns.

Unit of Measure

The units of measure (U/M) modify the quantities per assembly. A quantity of one (1) may be a box, pound, inch, or any of a long list of definitions. The unit of measure is one of the rules established on the master SKU level. Supply chain compliance issues dramatically affect units of measure by product within a customer. The unit of measure calculation methodology occasionally delays distribution ERP projects. Clearly understand your needs before starting the ERP search.

Sales Commissions

ERP systems contain codes for sales representatives and territories. Distributors frequently have complex commission formulas, but many packages lack the needed calculation methodology

Data, Files, Fields, and Codes

Files, fields, and system codes are mundane parts of the ERP selection process and seldom get attention until problems occur trying to implement the system. While not a leading cause for ERP failure, it contributes to delayed implementation. It is an obvious setback when discovering the system structure fails to support business needs.

Sales functionality for distribution companies is complicated. The customer order, not the item, connects the customer and the product. Each order contains all the nested item information. Distributors focus on completion of full orders instead of specific part numbers. A company needs to structure files and applications to manage by order and SKU. Complicating the issue, distribution companies on average have a greater number of SKUs packaged in multiple formats. A common practice is to break down a package with inventory and use the contents to complete an order.

Some data problems are:

- If the system is outdated, business requirements and software will be mismatched.

- If installing a new system, upgrade of current system or writing in house will consume significant time and resources.

- If installing a system for the first time, record preparation will be a major issue. All data and records require categorization, indexing, coding, cleansing, and data entry.

- If you are implementing a second or third-generation ERP, odds are high for data field sizes and calculation formula incompatibility. BOM offsets and ordering formulas are frequently out of date.

Manufacturing System

A Future State should include a review of production systems. The following layouts support manufacturing flows at a high-level conceptual view. Any planned changes to the shop floor normally occur in stages. The illustration iterates though a series of changes, each reducing inventory, increasing productivity and throughput, and collapsing order fulfillment time. Each system includes different ERP functionality. These are operational steps to the speed of reality equation.

Traditional Manufacturing

The first example shows a manufacturing flow often found in companies using simple methods. Inventory is "everywhere" and hot lists drive parts to queue final assembly. Thirty years ago, this was a prevalent layout found in most manufacturing operations. Expeditors chased parts commitments throughout operations, compiling a final assembly schedule that hopefully, but not necessarily, was in sequence with customer needs. Output drives the system, not priority. We call it "traditional," and this was the environment that ERP was designed to plan and manage. The lead-times were long and customer service (delivery to acknowledgement date), was frequently 85-90%. There are still manufacturing companies throughout the world operating in this environment. A modern ERP system will help, but traditional manufacturing plants frequently lack the internal discipline to make it work effectively.

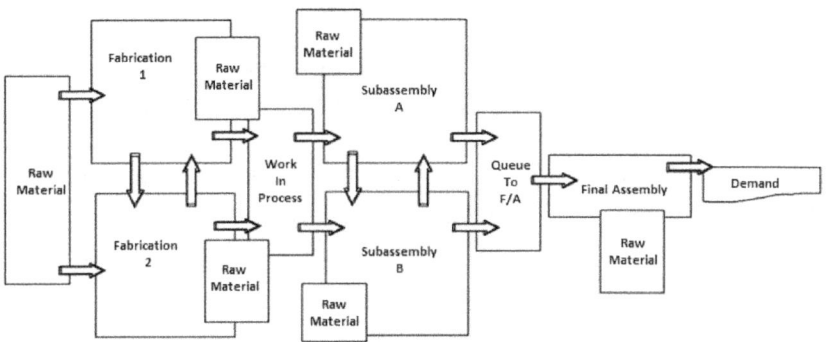

Illustration- Traditional repetitive manufacturing

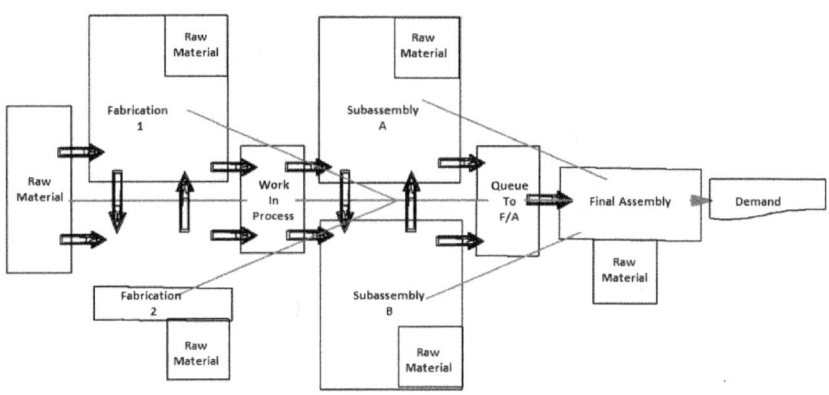

Illustration-Plant in transition

The second iteration is similar, but faced with increased pressure from customers and long purchase to cash cycles; manufacturing began working in different ways to increase throughput. One of these was driving the plant to customer priorities, made possible with ERP

77

systems. Management focused on shop flow, and reduced inventory by cutting queue times.

Companies with long lead times use safety stock formulas, inflating inventories by plan. These rules were (and still are) put into ERP systems, specifically those importing products from offshore manufacturers.

Concepts from the Toyota Production System

In the eighties, the Japanese continuous improvement concepts, primarily from the Toyota Production system (TPS), introduced a new set of manufacturing methodologies. We use three of these concepts, close coupling (clustering), Kanban, and cellular manufacturing to refine the plant layouts.

Close couple

Inventory is the bridge between disparate time requirements, whether between factory and customer, or operations on the shop floor. Moving facilities or machines closely together eliminates the need for inventory. TPS calls this close coupling, and Lean advocates label it "clustering."

Regardless of label, removing time and distance speeds up operations by reducing or eliminating move and queue time. It reduces inventory by cutting the time bridge. Both dramatically improve throughput and productivity.

Cellular Manufacturing

Old-school manufacturing sequenced machines and operators together to produce parts. The division of labor reduced work to smaller units where the operator(s) performs limited and specific tasks within the assigned three-square feet of responsibility.

Following is an example of parts produced in a sequential operation.

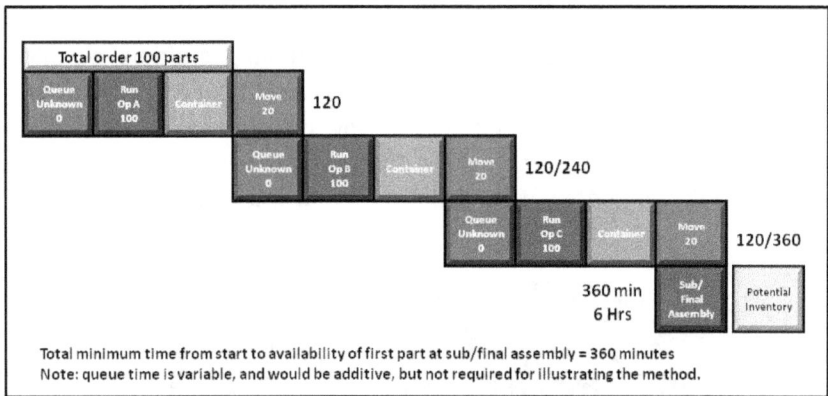

Illustration – Sequential process

One hundred parts, each rough machined at Operation A, go into a container. When all one hundred are completed, (less if there is scrap), they are queued (pushed) to the next operator. Completion occurs at Operation C. When the parts are finished, a fork truck takes the output container with one hundred parts to assembly operations.

Assuming each part takes one minute at each operation, the total run time is three hundred minutes. Assume the batch move time between operations is twenty minutes, totaling 60 minutes. The first part becomes available to the assembly operations in three hundred and sixty minutes or six hours.

In cellular production, the machines are organized (normally but not always), in a "U" shape per the illustration.

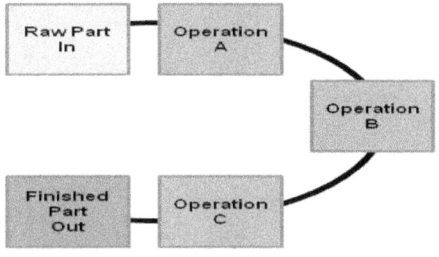

Illustration - Cellular process

One or more operators, each capable of running multiple machines, perform work within the cell. The raw parts are queued at Operation A. The part is processed and immediately given to the next operation and upon completion passes the part to Operation C. When done, the part is available (although not yet accessible) to final assembly.

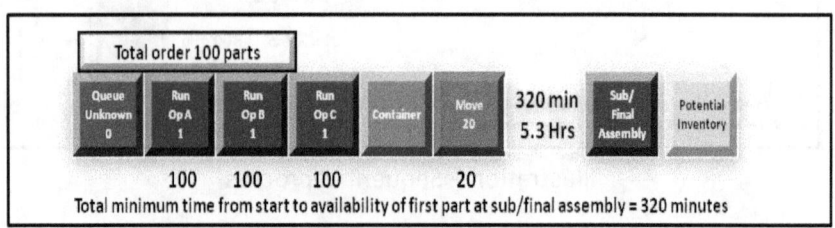

Assuming one minute per operation per part, the total time to produce one part from stop to finish is three minutes, with forty-minute savings in queue or move time. The distance and time a part or activity takes between completion and availability to the next operation is important. In the first two manufacturing layouts, parts go into inventory. The completed basket of parts is available to the next operation following the twenty minutes it takes to move the container from the final operation to assembly. Regardless, savings total forty minutes in queue time.

Kanban

Kanban is a system concept reengineered by Toyota into a useful and powerful planning and control mechanism. Conceptually, Kanban is a cycle, as shown in the next illustration.

KANBAN ROTATION

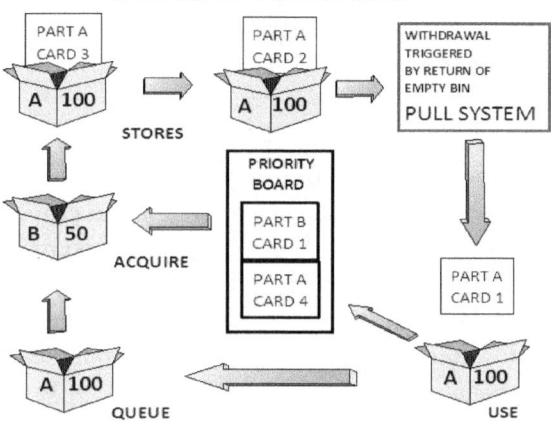

Illustration - Kanban

In Kanban, transactions and containers rotate between the user and the supplier. The cards (transactions) travel along with the containers and specify the quantity per container and other pertinent production information. When one card/unit is used, it cycles back to the supplier, representing demand for additional parts production.

The pull concept is a key Kanban feature. The using operation goes to the producing operation for the parts, or they may signal a need by presenting a card with an empty container. Production never pushes parts to the next operation, the case in most ERP systems. The Kanban transaction, card or electronic, triggers all activities.

In contemporary ERP systems, electronic signals replace the cards. Kanban requires specific order rules in the ERP system.

The number of open Kanban transactions in the system controls the total amount of inventory. The greater the requirements, the faster the replenishment demands on production, to produce higher frequency demands in a shorter production cycle.

Kanban presumes one to one (order) production lot sizes going into inventory. While zero inventories are a JIT concept, inventory is a tool of choice. Kanban employs a tightly controlled rotational inventory process.

Kanban has three major drawbacks. First, all container quantities have to be calculated. Second, manual Kanban systems are "blind" to ERP requirements. When an abnormally high-demand order hits the system, the Kanban may be under-planned. When demand drops, it takes time for the Kanban system to reflect the change. Third, Kanban works fine without reporting production or disbursements while ERP needs these transactions for accounting and material's planning. Bar coding Kanban transactions is one solution.

As manufacturing moves ever closer to "reality now" and demand-pull, everyone needs access to the information. The financial department and auditors must be involved in all discussions relevant to this issue.

Contemporary ERP systems incorporate Kanban functionality, processing and passing the requirements/changes in the background along with the relational calculations. The system calculates the Kanban transactions, recommending issues/recalls rotating through the shop.

There are applications where Kanban cards are superior to electronic methods, where low cost parts requirements are repetitive and highly predictable, but vary considerably in demand. Control is often loose and planning difficult. Putting the information on the cards saves the constant printing and distribution of orders, eliminating paper and electronic work schedules. Here is how one system works:

Using a rack, workers file the Kanban cards in priority sequence. The quantity has been predetermined and does not change. After using the parts in one Kanban container, the worker takes another to replace it. Refilling the empty container puts it in a queue, waiting for the demand (pull) signal.

There are circumstances where Kanban transactions are required to update the ERP system, but techniques reduce the pain of processing extra transactions. A bar-coding system, (see photo below) automates the process where planned production quantities equate to specific part numbers (SKU's).

Illustration - Kanban Visual System

The photograph is from a distributor client. The system was operational before we arrived, but it is classic. They used the system to manage an active less than case pack picking area with up to forty thousand SKU's. These cards rotated to the case pack storage area or kitting department for replenishment. This area was cycle counted and maintained a 98-99% record accuracy. While installing their new ERP system, the client modified the package and automated the highly successful techniques.

Other clients worked diligently to eliminate ERP and replace it with Kanban. While not entirely successful, they became highly sophisticated in applying the technique. They successfully extended the use of Kanban to manage a high percentage of their purchased parts and components, forming a partial demand pull system. In most cases, they have managed to avoid inventory, other than demand from the cards in the rotation, at both using and supplying plants. This eliminated purchase orders, receiving and incoming inspection, resulting in significant savings. All members of this collaboration are zealots for the system.

They achieve lot-to-lot Production, and the customer rarely runs short of components.

Future State – Demand Pull

Demand-pull is a JIT/Kanban derivative expanding the information integral to supply-chain management. (The illustration is on the next page.) Suppliers and customers share information about orders, product movement, and sales. If sales of a given product suddenly increase, that information flows back through each level of the supply chain. Each link has the information needed to adapt to changing conditions. The key focus of demand-pull is instant status/event sharing, giving all links more time to react.

While supply-chain management received little attention in this section, professionals heavily focus on the collaboration opportunities presented by demand flow. With this increased emphasis, discuss the concept internally, and if required, include the functionality in your future state design.

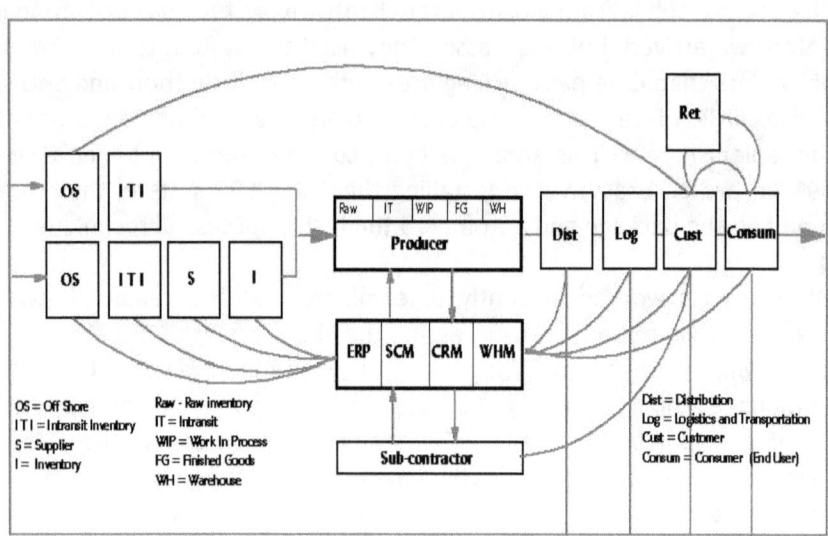

Illustration - Demand Flow

Kanban and demand flow are powerful tools for supply-chain management. Expanding the tool to demand pull increases its value. In any event, the cyclic and relational functions of JIT and ERP blend perfectly, making both stronger and more productive.

Applied TPS Concepts

In this example, operations are close coupled and the Cell operation directly feeds a small work-in-process area, providing the potential to take advantage of the three-minute parts availability from the manufacturing cell.

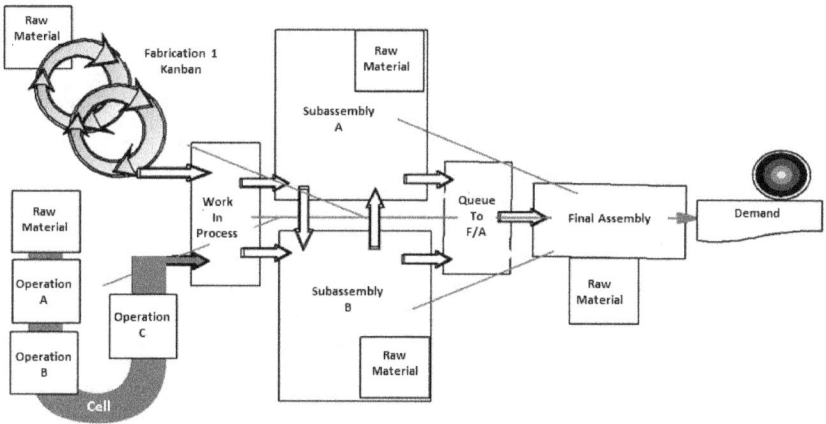

Illustration -Traditional Repetitive Manufacturing using cells and Kanban

Using Kanban and cellular production drastically reduces all inventories. These are special tools for dramatically increasing throughput and chopping lead-times.

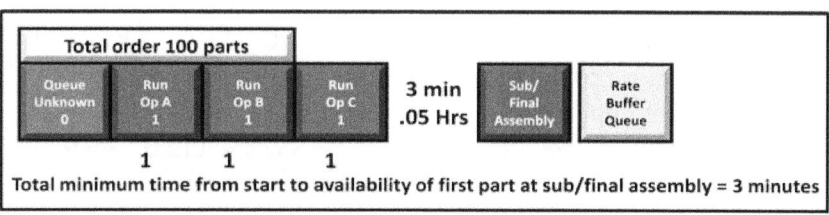

Synchronous Flow with Kanban and Manufacturing Cells

The system uses many of the concepts discussed throughout this manuscript. In this example, manufacturing cells feed a small work-in-process area, primarily to buffer different output rates. In carefully thought-out flows, production, and parts usage occurs rapidly, making inventory irrelevant. The following chart converts the above repetitive manufacturing process into a continuous flow layout using all the tools, including limited inventory.

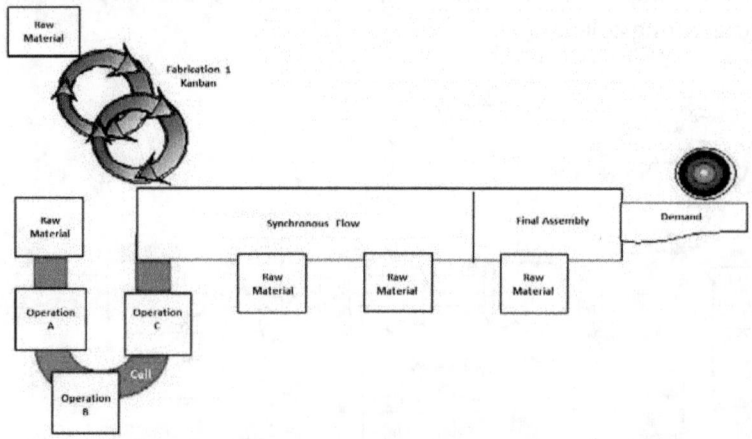

Illustration- Synchronous flow with Kanban and cells

This layout shows a close coupled, synchronous operation, virtually eliminating move times. The first finished part is now available in three minutes, and subsequent parts at one-minute intervals.

Following are the savings from close coupling and cell manufacturing.

	Minutes	Savings	Ratio
Traditional batch	360	0	
Cell (not close coupled)	320	40	12.5
Cell (close coupled)	3	317	105.7
Total	3	357	119.0

Understanding optional shop floor iterations allows the team to analyze software with the knowledge of a future plan. The four production layouts shown require increasingly sophisticated functionality.

Today, companies flatten bills of material, shorten lead-times, and work on programs with suppliers, such as JIT, to keep raw material at tight, hardworking levels. To accommodate these techniques, ERP incorporated JIT techniques, such as Kanban and demand pull.

Take-a-way

Spending time analyzing and rationalizing shop floor processes reflects a commitment to contemporary manufacturing techniques, including:

- ☐ Force multiplier concepts that drive all activities to the fulfillment of demand. The intent is to be demand driven using one-to-one manufacturing principles and pull concepts where possible.

- ☐ The utilization of the TPS concepts.

- ☐ ERP is normally thought of as a push method, but properly configured, it will pull assembly components from feeder departments (fabrication and subassembly), and raw materials required, to assembly planning.

- ☐ The system must handle subassembly operations with minimal work-in-process inventory.

- ☐ Use manufacturing cells where possible. Analyze flow throughout the value chain and determine cell potential. Ensure the ERP has the needed functionality to manage cells with schedules and techniques for planning, loading, and reporting.

- ☐ Use electronic and card Kanban systems where applicable. The Kanban cycle potentially extends into the supplier's inventory and into the customer's warehouse.

Until manufacturing is using all the available tools to compress time, faster information may prove to be an expense. Take the time to plan for fast, accurate physical and information realities. The task may require multiple steps, re-engineering, ERP tools, and VMP.

Distribution System

All of these principles apply equally to distribution. Following is a visualization of the distribution system, as planned after application of the TPS concepts. This chart details the facility layout and the required systems features.

- ☐ Directed put away at receiving
- ☐ Directed order picking using multiple picking methods
- ☐ Less than case pack forward picking areas replenished from full case pack area
- ☐ ERP controlled components storage for kitting area
- ☐ Modifications
- ☐ Kanban for kitted inventory replenishment and to fill "less than case pack" orders
- ☐ Flow-through quality control checks
- ☐ Case pack area
- ☐ Cross docking
- ☐ Shipment staging to plan

Additional features are:

- ☐ Directed picking by order number, not just SKU
- ☐ Preplanned transportation
- ☐ Load optimization

Distribution Layout

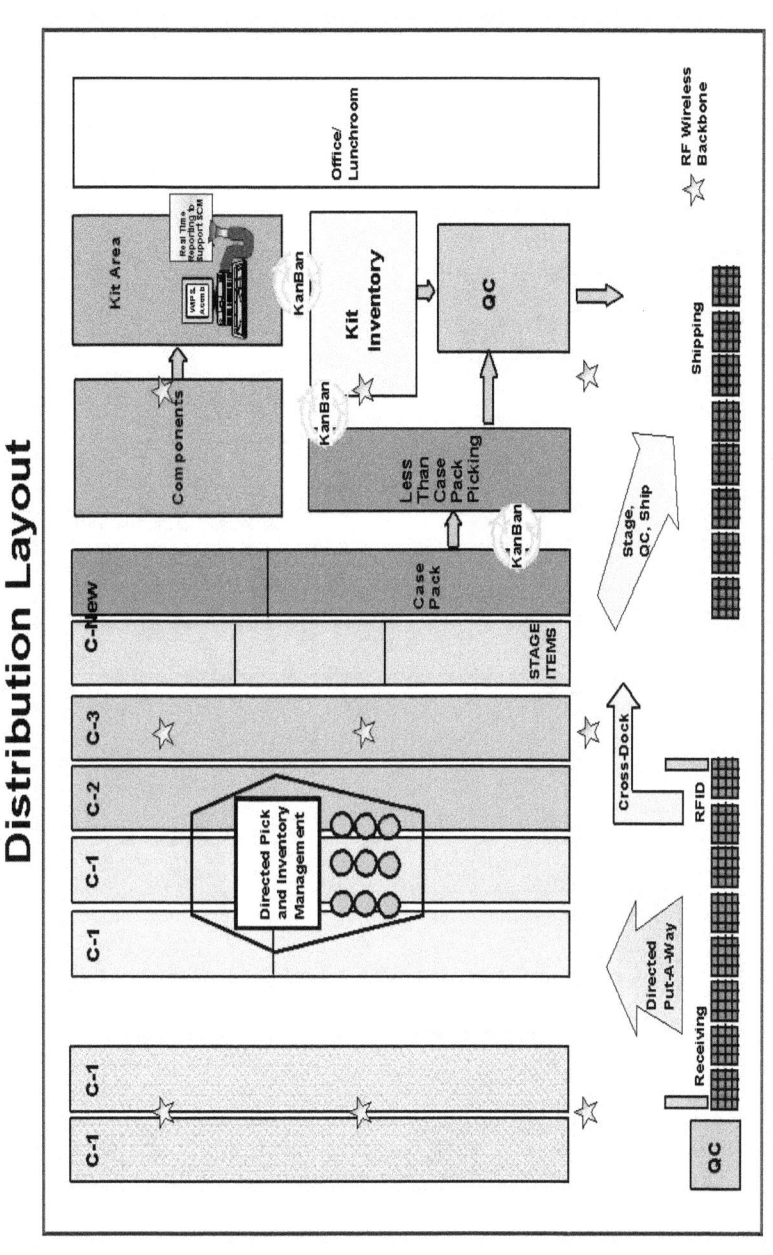

Illustration - Distribution Layout

An additional distribution issue is customer specified packaging.

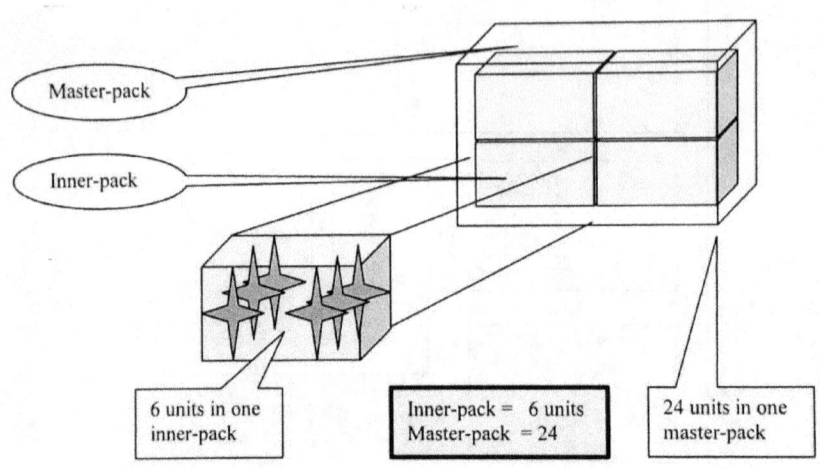

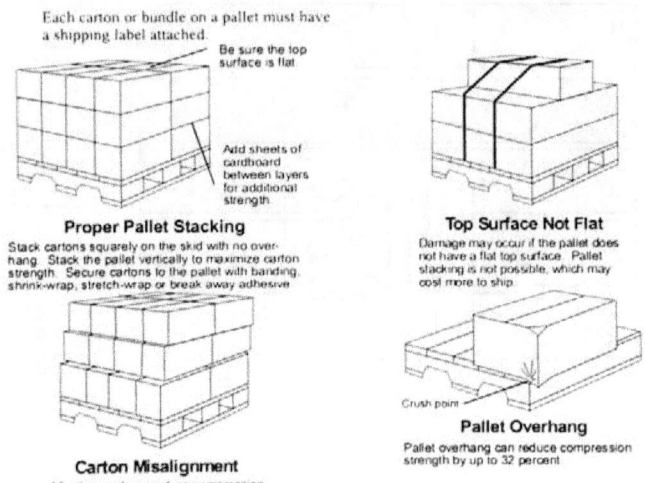

Be very specific about packaging requirements and the effect on ERP selection.

Supply Chain

ERP software packages, designed primarily to plan and manage internal resources, provide varying key components of supply-chain management and collaboration. Like manufacturing and distribution, supply chains must receive detail attention in both the assessment and future state phases.

SCM incorporates elements of purchasing, logistics, and materials, and touches every part of the enterprise. In many companies, records reside on the ERP system and on one or more personal computers.

The key is to build fast, tight, integrated supply chains. In summary, the objectives are:

- One integrated system instead of disparate chunks
- Tightly synchronize demand/supply cycles
- Make the supply chains productive and predictable
- Reduce the risk of supply interruption
- Reduce the risk of cost fluctuations
- Prepare for continued pressure on purchasing products from non-polluting sources
- Avoid paying for supplier's inefficiencies

For the purposes of the future state, there are additional issues.

Two conceptual themes are JIT/Kanban and close coupling, both covered earlier. Generally, international supply chains violate both concepts. Implicit are opportunities for compressing time, tighter inventory management, and faster response to changing customer needs.

The following illustration shows a domestic supply chain across the top and the international supply chain as a loop. Write the lead-time for each element in your organization. Compare the lead-times and dollarize the effects.

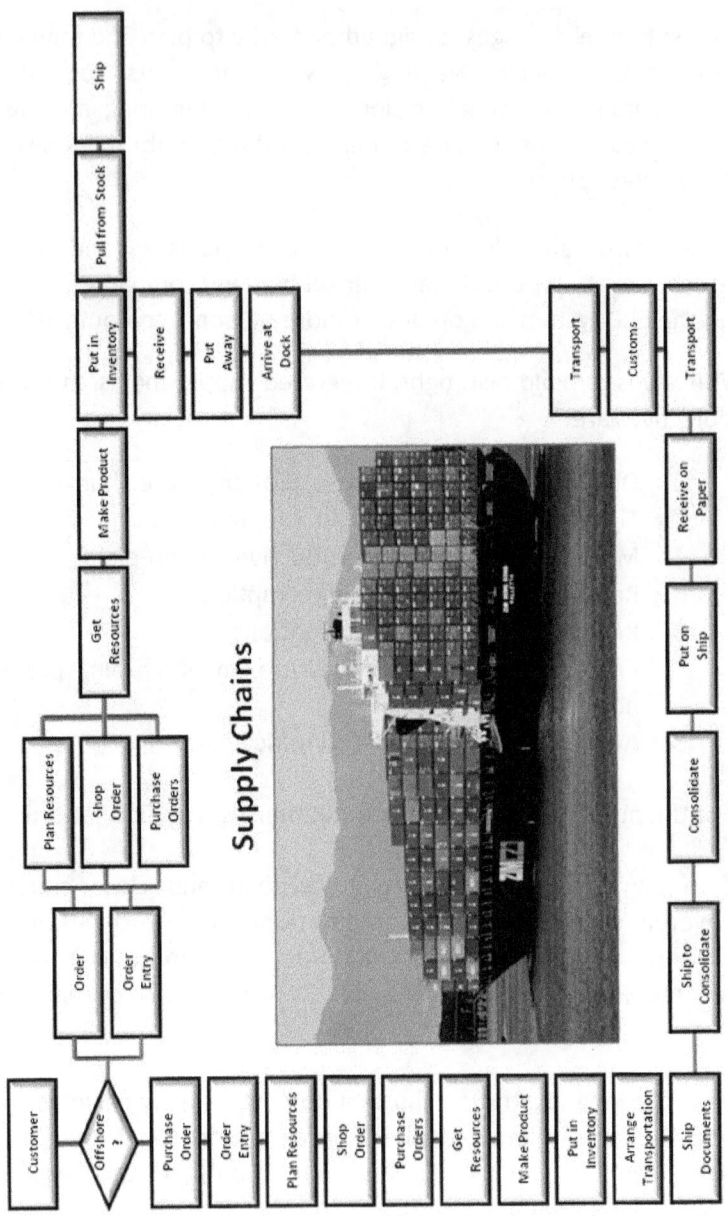

Illustration- Domestic vs. International Supply Chains

In effect, products purchased instead of manufactured use capital differently. SCM invests in relationships, while domestic production may invest in productive capacity.

The lesson learned is the need to recalculate the true cost of outsourcing, and if re-sourcing is a better alternative, factor the necessary actions into the future state.

Process Improvement (VMP)

ERP selection is normally divorced from process improvement. In many important ways, the programs complement each other but compete for resources. Both improve the performance of the organization and require high corporate priorities, are team based, consume valuable resources during implementation and are expensive. Properly done both are cost effective. Poorly done, either can cripple the business.

The classical definition of productivity is "output per hour worked." A more comprehensive definition will factor in effectiveness.

"Productivity is the use of time, technology, and resources, effectively adding value to goods and/or services."

The Just-in-Time (JIT), Lean Six Sigma attitude fixated on speed, efficiency and the elimination of non-value adding activities, summarized as waste. Cutting time reduces inventory requirements, improves productivity, and drives up customer service. It increases the focus on operational priorities, doing the right thing, building the correct product and doing it on time. Contemporary lean programs will intensify the focus on methods to increase yield and optimize resources.

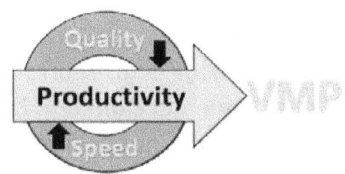

Value Management Program

Illustration: Cycle of Quality and Speed

Many VMP initiatives wind up being cost reduction efforts, sacrificing quality for short-term financial purposes. Any program to improve processes must include stringent quality standards, or it will devalue the product, process, or implementation.

Quality and speed must not become a paradox. Doing the wrong thing faster is not productive nor does poor quality add value. Process speed should never exceed the ability to produce quality results. The speed of reality includes information and process, both done with high quality.

The result of any VMP is to add value to the company, its products, and customer service. For those reasons, the term "value management programs" (VMP) more accurately defines the overall objective.

Any properly conducted search for the contemporary business reality will factor business transformation methodology into the equation. The study may indicate that culture change must precede a new ERP system. A changing business model may indicate a more complicated or time phased approach to several types of business solutions. It is becoming more obvious that companies applying VMP methodologies for software projects install systems faster and at lower cost.

VMP is an important component of any ERP project in two forms. If done prior to selecting the ERP software, it may change the functional requirements. In turn, the new ERP infrastructure can facilitate the savings promised by Lean. ERP implies changing business processes, and realizing a return on investment (ROI) requires business process changes. Any type of business may use visual or Lean techniques, and Lean companies frequently use ERP in innovative ways.

Short, rapid reaction capabilities are ideal outcomes, and real time systems may be more expensive but dramatically change business adaptability. For these reasons, VMP and information technology are partners. They both compress time and speed up business. Automation is the third component of speed, and needs to be part of the planned future state.

When selecting an ERP product, match your information and physical reality time. Make sure the future state system will be fast enough to support needed adaptability. Speed is an order winner and profit driver.

Project Plan-High Level

The Future Vision is part of the critical path and establishes a reasoned planning process to develop tactics and action items supporting strategy and operations. The project plan is the first step in establishing the project structure. In many ways, the first pass is a matrix of activities and situations.

Charting the shape of the business, visualization and process designs help define the ERP type. The documentation serves two purposes. The first use is to clarify internal information. The second is to reduce the number of potential ERP suppliers. A supplier shown these documents will quickly determine if their software products fulfill your specifications. The inability to prepare visualization means the solution may still be fuzzy and requires additional definition or refinement.

There are significant unknowns at the initial stage of the plan, and details will come into focus as the project matures. One example is the ERP supplier's implementation process. As new inputs become available, layer the actionable issues into the plan matrix.

This plan requires strategic definitions, business case/process designs, and a preliminary schedule for the selection process. It includes training the team on ERP selection techniques, and presents the business case for a new ERP system. A schedule of events with estimated timing is required. If the study indicates a pervasive resistance to change, include recommendations for a transformation process. For example, training on change management, focused on a positive process.

Using your chosen project management software, assign initial due dates to all activities. They will change as specific relationships and timing between events becomes available. Take the opportunity to detail the critical project organization steps, including how crewing issues will be resolved.

Conduct review sessions with all associates involved in the study to validate the accuracy of the data, process designs, and the conclusions. Address all of their needs. Conduct a project approval meeting with the executive staff. Establish a budget, assign a priority, and properly staff the program.

To streamline the approval process, obtain estimates. Prepare a spreadsheet showing the time phased expenditure for equipment, software, and consultants. Prepare a recommendation section. This will provide a first cut plan for managing the financial aspect of the project.

Conceptual Systems Design

- Translation of strategy into ERP terms
- Analysis of the gap between strategy and capability
- A conceptual plan to bridge the gap
- A technology integration plan to support the conceptual plan
- Project recommendations and options - a formal plan in outline form
- Suggested priorities
- Rough-cut financial impact

Statement of the System's Objectives (examples)

- Use Lean Six Sigma methodologies throughout the organization
- 24-hour shipment on 90% of the orders
- One-minute visibility of all orders and quotes
- Rapid prototyping/sampling to support sales efforts
- 98% on-time delivery as measured by completed orders
- The elimination of an annual physical inventory
- Inventory turns increased by two turns each year with less than 2% stock outs
- Productivity improved by a 15% average for the next five years
- All records of the business maintained at 98% accuracy
- Cycle time cut until it is equal to customer lead-time
- Fully integrated financial reporting
- One to one production where needed

- ☐ High velocity, highly flexible manufacturing capability
- ☐ Supply chains with full, real-time access to information
- ☐ Collaboration programs supporting product design and Lean Six Sigma
- ☐ Define potential and costs for future outsourcing and reshoring
- ☐ Develop a convergence plan for information and process
- ☐ Install ERP system as infrastructure
- ☐ Install other software when the ERP system is operational
- ☐ Rapid but limited product modification in the distribution centers
- ☐ Redefinition of product numbers (SKU's) to facilitate sales over the Internet
- ☐ Development of group technology codes
- ☐ Use of cells
- ☐ Develop systems/methods to eliminate shop and distribution paperwork

Integration Plan

This plan interprets and time phases the conceptual plan into hardware and ERP requirements. Until the selection process is completed, some of the details will be unavailable. If known, the plan states what and when to acquire and install hardware, and identify the associated training.

The distribution and shop layout examples identify different technologies, including bar coding, RFID, Kanban, equipment moves, and mobile technologies. They support the strategic plans and the implementation of the ERP system. The timing and expenses are scheduled. Each step has a subordinate implementation plan.

Information systems hardware is a major component of the integration plan. At this level, the plan often is a matrix because the issue is undefined. For those companies that know their systems configuration, it is the addition of technology to support the future state.

Server Platform

Your new software will run on a given set of hardware/software platforms. These optionally include IBM (AS/400, iSeries, System i), Linux (SUSE, Red Hat, Debian/Ubuntu), UNIX (Solaris or AIX), Microsoft server (Windows, NT/2003/Vista/Win8), Novell Netware, and hosted solutions such as SaaS.

The platform must be determined as part of the software selection process if not known prior to starting the software search. If the decision is to use current platforms, it defines one selection parameter. Delegate the hardware issues to your IT department, who will know the implications of making changes. If you lack an IT department, consider hiring a hardware consultant. An informed decision is required before, during and after the selection process.

Dialog once centered on the different capabilities of Windows and UNIX. Our firm has always favored the IBM platform because it is highly reliable and less susceptible to hackers, virus, and downtime. Personal computers function independently or in networks. The software license applies to one or more PCs. Carefully think through the implications of non-integrated information inherent with PCs.

As you narrow the search for software, the rule is to ask what the native platform is. Some software is not hardware dependent, and many suppliers provide software for more than one platform.

Following is a partial list of considerations:

- ☐ Resolve centralized vs. decentralized processing
- ☐ Hardware platform
- ☐ Operating System
- ☐ Open source – Linux
- ☐ UNIX
- ☐ Microsoft
- ☐ Network plan, e.g. distributed
- ☐ PCs and software
- ☐ Mobile devices and supporting technologies

- ☐ Need to address non-solution issues
- ☐ Availability of security and data
- ☐ Remote support requirements
- ☐ Integration with other systems
- ☐ Telephone/Fax
- ☐ Machine and process tools and software interface
- ☐ Support tools
- ☐ Known process changes
- ☐ Key phases with estimated completion dates
- ☐ Mobile communications integration
- ☐ Systems Impact Considerations
- ☐ Other economies achieved/lost
  - ☐ Air conditioning
  - ☐ Technological rollover
  - ☐ Keeping up to date
  - ☐ Security
  - ☐ Disaster recovery
  - ☐ Ongoing costs
  - ☐ Multi-layering, usability
  - ☐ Cabling, electrical
  - ☐ Systems / server space, noise, heat
  - ☐ Support personnel needed
  - ☐ Networks of PC required
  - ☐ Upgrades frequency
  - ☐ Cost factor

Summary

Systems projects are complex and failure has consequences. Having an intimate knowledge of the playing field (business), the game (processes), the reward (project success), and the consequences are vital. Take the time to develop a rock-solid future state and the subordinate plans to achieve it.

Step 4 Decision to Achieve the Future State

The assessment, future state, and project plans are iterative processes with a number of opportunities for management review. For some initiatives, it is a late cycle planning event. Executive management may have decided the direction, to focus on ERP solutions or Lean Six Sigma or both. This is a structured approach, abet an event-driven process, and the next logical step is to review, modify and approve the plan.

Executive Review of the Plan

The project team and consultants formally present the Future State to the executive staff, who must freely question any area of concern. This needs to be a moment of intense transparency by all parties.

Preliminary Budget -Estimated

- ☐ Time phased expenses synchronized to actions
- ☐ Internal personnel
- ☐ Consulting fees
- ☐ ERP software costs
- ☐ Maintenance fees
- ☐ Hardware (Technology Integration Plan)
- ☐ Training
- ☐ Estimate process changes
- ☐ Other out of pocket

Return on Investment (ROI)

The future state contains recommendations and is a working document used to keep associates involved, current and in agreement. Until the specific project costs are determined, the ROI is preliminary, and updates are required.

- ☐ Understand what comprises the ROI. It will probably be overstated and unobtainable without process improvements. Has the team defined the changes?

- ☐ ROI requires continuous improvement. The system builds the infrastructure to achieve effectiveness. VMP makes the change required to increase velocity, achieve agility and effectiveness, lower cost and to increase profits.

- ☐ Most implementations do not yield immediate paybacks, with the Lean program providing the majority of the ROI. Project the cost and benefits over three years. Show base savings on the third year, not the first.

- ☐ The team must focus on productivity improvements, legitimate cost saving and/or improved service and profitability. It may simply be a case of building the infrastructure for a VMP, or because you need a new system "to stay in business."

- ☐ Advise the team not to use headcount reductions for the ROI. They seldom occur as planned and may be detrimental if the project includes the process improvement step. If reductions are included, get specific positions from the team. Tell them the cuts will be part of the measurement for program success. Give the team members an opportunity to change their minds.

- ☐ Do not use "funny money." Executive management and the Board will know exactly what is going on and question each number, both legitimate and funny money.

- ☐ Update the time-phased project plan developed in the future state. Convert the plan into a high-level PERT/GANT chart (normally part of the project management software) to illustrate benchmark activities. This effort has planned completion dates, including contingency buffers. Check and double-check all offsets.

- ☐ Spell out
  - ☐ Benefits
  - ☐ Risks of doing or not doing
  - ☐ Scope
  - ☐ Hardware required
  - ☐ RF System and/or RFID

- ☐ The review will include:
  - ☐ The Future State
  - ☐ Project Plan
  - ☐ Subordinate plans to accomplish the Future State
    - ☐ The Technology Integration Plan
    - ☐ The Detail Project Plan
  - ☐ Project recommendations and options
  - ☐ Suggested priorities
  - ☐ Thorough preliminary financial impact
  - ☐ Options for on-premise, cloud solution, or hybrid

Project Review

- ☐ Project team meets with the executive staff and reviews the plan, benefits and ROI
- ☐ Ask the really tough questions

Decisions

Given these inputs, executive management must decide on the future course of action. These include:

- ☐ Do nothing

- ☐ Business transformation
- ☐ Implement an enterprise system: ERP, WHMS, CRM, SCM, MES, BI and which components will be on-premise or off
- ☐ Implement a business VMP.
- ☐ Accelerate convergence
- ☐ Outsource (requires detail plan)
- ☐ In source (requires detail plan)
- ☐ Export
- ☐ Review other business opportunities isolated during the review
- ☐ Commit the dollars for thorough organizational training. If the money is not available, cancel or delay the project.

Given a decision to implement an ERP system, the following is a subset of associated decisions dealing with how to accomplish the project. For example:

- ☐ Purchase ERP software
- ☐ Fix the current system
- ☐ Reinstall
- ☐ Apply upgrades
- ☐ ASP/SaaS or other cloud option
- ☐ Rewrite in-house
- ☐ VMP as first step
- ☐ VMP as a follow-up program

Summary

If executive management does not like the plan or lacks the resources to make it happen, it is a waste of time working through the selection and justification process. It is essential, once approved, to get all associates on the same page.

Given the decision, the project must receive a priority, budget, and a commitment to resources.

Step 5 Organize for the project

Successful programs are well organized. This may seem obvious, but installing ERP is a disruptive process generating some level of chaos before restoring order by successfully completing the system. If unsuccessful, the chaos continues and broadens. Meanwhile, the business has to operate while working on the program.

The lesson learned is that all projects encounter difficult situations. Anticipation and vigilance are critical issues, and now is the time to plan and develop a well-reasoned approach to problem resolution. It is executive management's responsibility to take every step to remove ambiguity.

Executive

Examine the project PERT/GANT Chart and question every detail. Understand how long the project will take then add a generous chunk of time for miscalculation. The most probable guarantee is it will take longer than anyone's estimates, and it will consume more resources. The quality of the planning activity and team/organization training greatly increase the odds of being on time and within budget.

The first issue is a level of commitment, starting at the top. Every executive will make significant contributions to the program. This may be staff assigned, delaying pet projects, or the transfer of power into the project. The executive staff must walk the talk and understand their accountability for poor progress in areas of responsibility. While middle management and shop supervision will be the most actively involved, they cannot do the job without support from their functional executives. Each of the following summarized points is detailed on subsequent pages.

- ☐ The President/CEO must be committed and if not, stop the program.
- ☐ Take careful steps to get buy-in by the executive staff, middle management, line, and user communities.
- ☐ Have a change management class to help people adapt, learn new methods, and follow protocols.
- ☐ Provide appropriate incentives.

Team Formation
- ☐ Executive Steering Committee
- ☐ Executive Champion
- ☐ Project Leader
- ☐ Project Team
- ☐ External consultant

Clearly spell out associate's role and the proper chain of command
- ☐ Explain expectations
- ☐ Provide a plan
- ☐ Provide a budget
- ☐ Establish a high priority

Outline the reporting timing and method
- ☐ Monthly project report to President/CEO and the Board
    - ☐ Provide all the necessary resources
        - ☐ A dedicated team or employee backfill
        - ☐ Hire consultants where necessary
        - ☐ Provide a "War Room."

Allocate training dollars and facilities

ERP projects are high-priority projects, so avoid giving associates conflicting priorities. You will fail! When everything is a priority, nothing is a priority. Is the project priority high enough to get the job done? If not, stop the process or change the priority – and back it. Keep the priority problems in the boardroom and out of the project.

Work issues

Management must decide how to deal with work issues. Disruptive events can occur when key people are on the project team.

The team members often do their regular jobs while installing the new system. Prepare to add help if daily tasks suffer. In most companies, it is impractical to completely backfill team members because of talents, experience, skill sets, and their importance to the business.

Systems are not cheap and money must be available for extra people. Following are places where temporary help may be useful.

- Data conversion/data entry
- Procedures/documentation
- Clerical support

Temporary employment firms offer support at virtually any level. We have enjoyed excellent results using University and Technical School students, with majors including IT, engineering, process engineering, and teachers. They were smart and willing workers.

- The team members will normally find a way to get critical daily functions completed. If they cannot deal with the increased workload, then rethink the composition of the team.

- Provide full information access to the associates.

- Hire temporary help when needed.

- Run interference when needed to overcome roadblocks.

Appoint the Executive Steering Committee

The team is established level-by-level. First, the President/CEO appoints the steering committee and the executive champion or sponsor. They are empowered to make the decisions for the project. The executive champion must be one of the members, and the President/CEO frequently fills the role as another. The President/CEO, depending upon the size of the company, may participate in the selection of the project team manager and the members of the cross-functional project team.

Their duties of the Executive Steering Committee are:

- Court of appeals
- Review scope and progress
- Review and approve decisions
- Resolve cross-organizational conflicts
- Define key business drivers and critical processes
- Project approval / contract issues
- The big picture – rise above the detail
- Provide priority
- Assess / resolve personnel issues
- Provide / resolve resource contention
- Project oversight
- Budget tracking approval:
    - Project changes
    - Process changes

Appoint the Executive Champion

The prime requirement for the executive champion is good leadership skills. Normally viewed in technical terms, installing and making ERP systems work are people issues. The most useful skills are project management, followed by ERP knowledge, and good communications skills. The role of the executive champion is:

- Get company support for the team throughout the organization

- [ ] Keep the project on the management agenda
- [ ] Make the tough executive-level project decisions
- [ ] Help sell and implement project needs
- [ ] Act as project conscience and sounding board
- [ ] Retain:
  - [ ] Open-door policy
  - [ ] Solve problems not fire or punish people
  - [ ] Refuse to duck the problems
  - [ ] Resolve conflicts when the Project Manager is unable to fix them (may involve the Project Manager)
  - [ ] Own the process
- [ ] Establish and implement a security program
- [ ] Act as security change authorization control point
- [ ] Establish rules and expectations
- [ ] Define the need for and the role of a consultant/facilitator along with the executive steering committee
- [ ] Appropriate reporting level for outside consultants
- [ ] Provide a war room for the project team

Outside Consultant

Decide on the use of an outside consultant to help with the process. Our experience indicates that consultants should not be the project manager. External project leaders cause authority conflicts, contention between team and ERP consultants (if different). At the end of the project, they go home while internal personnel must live with the results.

The exception to these guidelines is contracting the entire project to a consulting firm. Here are some tips for working with consultants.

- [ ] Define reporting relationships.
- [ ] Define the scope.
- [ ] The consultant should be completely free of financial relationships to ERP suppliers. The objective is to find the right ERP for your company.
- [ ] Be very specific about compensation and billable events.

The advantages of a consultant are:

- [ ] Provide a structured approach, much like this one.
- [ ] They have expertise at selecting and installing ERP systems.
- [ ] Since they know the pitfalls, they can provide early warnings and direction.
- [ ] They are impartial
- [ ] Getting at the root cause
- [ ] Focusing on the right applications
- [ ] Finding the right ERP
- [ ] Ensuring there is an executable implementation plan
- [ ] Act in support of project manager/executive champion

The decision to retain a consultant is contingent on project requirements. The executive champion may decide to use a consultant as a control against the software company.

- [ ] Facilitate planning
- [ ] Follow up to make sure of activity completion
- [ ] Assist Project Manager preparing and making reports
- [ ] Help resolve the technical issues
- [ ] Eyes and ears for executive management

Immediately upon project completion, the contract is closed. Extend or rewrite the contact for additional work if justified.

Select the Project Manager

A recent trend was to make rookie IT people the ERP Project Leader. This reflects a serious lack of understanding the complexities encountered during an ERP project. The Project Leader must be someone with both project and leadership skills. They may not have full knowledge of ERP systems, but the right consultant can help fill this gap. It is virtually impossible to overcome all the challenges a rookie will encounter, and it our recommendation that any organization that has taken this step seriously reconsiders the exposure they are subjecting the business too. Properly used, rookies can be tomorrow's stars, but they need a chance to learn and succeed. It serves no useful purpose to turn them off early in their careers.

Determine who the Project Leader will be:

- The CIO is the first, logical choice
- It should not be a consultant (with previously noted exceptions) – need in-house authority
- It should be a strong internal person
- Someone who gets things done
- Knowledge of the ERP concepts and business processes is essential
- Non-information technology leaders are often effective
- If process changes are significant, an operation's person may be a better choice
- Project management training/skills are a plus

Responsibilities:

- Manage and control the project – leadership – day to day
- Resolve all issues
- Immerse in detail when required
- No shortcut mentality – do it right
- Schedule and follow-up on all activities
- Maintain schedule integrity
- Rigorous follow up on the parking lot list
- Training
- Coordinate activities, events and reports with the team, executive team, and executive champion, outside consultant and software/hardware suppliers
- Communicate system impact issues
- Promote, participate, and follow up on team and user training
- Perform or participate in the gap analysis (between the old and the new system)

- ☐ Rigorously manage and control any/all data conversion and migration processes
- ☐ Progress assessment
- ☐ Preparation of the request for proposal
- ☐ Be involved with the vendor partnering process
- ☐ ERP software selection
- ☐ Contribute input into the negotiation process
- ☐ Manage the implementation and migration to the new system
- ☐ Support ongoing operations
- ☐ Insure high-quality project documentation
- ☐ Establish and control all go-live processes
- ☐ Ensure testing / user acceptance
- ☐ Follow-up on all post-implementation problems

Establish the Teams

The team members are normally managerial or supervisory. It is important that team members involve their subordinates in a functional team format.

Team formation – select the team members – these must be some of the best people in the organization.

- ☐ They must be decision-makers and experts in their areas
- ☐ Communicators, but doers, not talkers
- ☐ They must know the job processes
- ☐ Know how and where of take shortcuts without causing adverse effects
- ☐ They must be open minded
- ☐ Dedicated to fight for the best business solution and then making it work
- ☐ Savvy to the inner-working of the company
- ☐ Has or can quickly acquire needed technical skills
- ☐ Willing to participate in making the final selection

111

People need to be open-minded and work as a team. Do not ignore the dissenters; especially associates expert in their area. Do not mistake a cry for help or a warning as being anti-project.

Technical Persons

Internal and external technical people are required. These members need a combination of good technical skills and communication skills. Their role is:

- ☐ Active participation in all project phases
- ☐ Ensure hardware and software compatibility
- ☐ Implement technical changes
- ☐ Control all program modifications and validate conformance to specifications and needs
- ☐ Make changes tailored to the business needs
- ☐ Explain costs and options
- ☐ Lead data conversion / migration effort
- ☐ Participate in "cloud" application appraisals and decisions
- ☐ Strong voice in platform selection
- ☐ Take the lead on all hardware requirement's definition, acquisition and installation
- ☐ Ensure application of system codes
- ☐ Oversee password protocols and security assignments
- ☐ Protect the integrity of converted data and files
- ☐ Ensure maintenance of current systems until the decision is made to shift all support to the new system

End Associates

A cross-functional team is comprised of supervisors and key personnel from the user community. Some companies call them captains. Associates reporting to the team members must often perform the work, becoming functional implementation teams. Fold these often-informal teams into the communication loops by holding frequent meetings with these team members, who will do most of the detail work. Keeping the functional team motivated will determine the success of the project.

Functional teams are the unsung heroes and the source of pragmatic solutions, so train all associates. End associates:

- ☐ Know where and how to put efforts
- ☐ Know the processes
- ☐ Know where and how to develop functional workarounds
- ☐ Must want to do the job well
- ☐ Must work with the chosen solution
- ☐ Associates will quickly determine if a process is user friendly

Vendors

Multiple vendors will play critical roles in the implementation, including the software and hardware suppliers, possible third parties, and data collection/network providers. Since the life cycle of an ERP system may be "years," it is important that support personnel work well together.

- ☐ Honest relationship built on trust
- ☐ Provide quality products fulfilling the business needs
- ☐ Assist in education
- ☐ Assist in the solution setup
- ☐ Streamline
- ☐ Custom options
- ☐ Hook to other legacy applications
- ☐ Product expertise
- ☐ They must work with each other

Team meeting

The President/CEO, Executive Champion, and Steering Committee must brief the teams on expectations and business strategies. In most cases, the team will guard against mismatches if known.

- ☐ Future process changes – review the Future State.

- ☐ Discuss future markets
- ☐ Discuss future opportunities
- ☐ Share critical financial data to build trust
- ☐ Discuss the need to keep the business running efficiently during the project
- ☐ Outline the reporting structure
- ☐ Spell out expectations

Reporting

Define the reporting method for updating the steering committee and the Board of Directors. Spell out the frequency of reports and the distribution list.

The decision

Who will make the ERP decision? With a package selected, the team will take a consensus vote to confirm the ERP package. Will the vote stick or will the executive staff override the decision?

Putting the project plan into place

Update the project plan with specific assignments and responsibilities.

Initial team training

Team training on the following subjects is required before the selection process can start.

- ☐ A functional review of the business
- ☐ Change management
- ☐ The fundamentals of ERP
- ☐ The fundamentals of Lean as applied to ERP selection
- ☐ ERP evaluation methodology
- ☐ How to evaluate the packages and what to guard against

Training

Executive management needs to commit to train well and thoroughly. We use the analogy of a 747. An airline does not buy an expensive and sophisticated aircraft and then train its pilots to a basic visual status. It is difficult to understand why enterprises fail to implement training programs and take full advantage of the comprehensive functionality in the ERP system.

Lean Six Sigma principles relate to ERP program applications. Any potential functionality paid for but unrealized is a waste. Not training, or using all the training dollars is another false economy. It is amazing how many companies fail to grasp this basic principle. If the enterprise is not going to spend the money training the teams and associates, executive management should seriously consider delaying or canceling the project until ready to make that commitment. To take advantage of ERP capabilities, train everyone, including management.

Phased rollout vs. Big Bang

ERP implementations take two basic forms. The first is a phased rollout, where the cutover occurs module by module per a time phased schedule. Nearly all-large enterprises follow this practice since it would be too disruptive and difficult to control if all cutovers occurred at once.

The second approach is the Big Bang. All the work leads up to a one-time cut over, which normally takes place over a weekend at the end of a month. The decision of phased versus big bang may not be possible until the inputs from the ERP supplier are available. Cut over timing is an important consideration and deserves due diligence. Discuss the decision at a steering committee meeting.

A third method, parallel adoption (an adaptation of the phased rollout) occurs by module, business unit, or geographical location. This method applies to enterprises installing a pilot corporate system, and then implementing the system in other plants.

Establish a Data Conversion Methodology

Data conversion can be the longest Critical Path item and of greater complexity than anticipated. Unrealistic pressure to meet the deadline results in poor conversion, creating negative effects as data problem's plaque the implementation. The responsibility for data conversion, how and who will do it must be determined early in the project. Mapping current data to the new system must wait until the software selection.

Part numbers may be changed. Group technology codes assigned, and descriptions changed for Internet sales or multi-company codes applied. While delegated to the technical personnel, it is important for the Project Manager and Executive champion to meet daily and review the progress, then implement actions

Define and establish the change process

Establish a change control process and make the Project Manager responsible. Changes must be justified, documented, and backed up with an impact analysis.

The steering committee and project leader will overview and manage allowable changes. While the implementation plan is in itself a series of changes, other opportunities or problems will surface during execution. Issues affecting the time-line and budget must go through a justification process, analysis, and a priority assigned.

Documented, but excluded changes represent potential opportunities for a VMP, the last step in the process.

We recommend using "ACTION," the VMP/change management methodology explained in the last chapter, "Continuous Improvements - Perfect the System".

Establish a general philosophy on program modifications

It is useful to establish a policy stating there will be no modifications without the approval of the steering committee. Communicate this

116

direction to the team, and then vigorously enforce it. The alternative is to find the best match, work-a-round or process change. Once achieved, document it, define the cost, and execute it within the parameters of the project, but only with the approval of the steering committee.

We recommend reviewing the section on "Parking Lot Lists, Modifications, and Middleware."

Because it is unreasonable to expect a precise match to the requirements, there will always be a gap necessitating program modifications of some type. People will have to change the way they view and process information, and reports modified to perform differently.

Make Business Continuity Plans

- ☐ Disaster-recovery plans
- ☐ Backup and restore plans
- ☐ Documentation
- ☐ Change management
- ☐ Implement service level agreement
- ☐ Technical services
- ☐ Management
- ☐ End associates

Report to the Executive Staff and Board of Directors

Given a properly prepared plan, extracting a summary for executive management or the Board of Directors becomes an easy, automated process.

- ☐ Review the Future Vision
  - ☐ Present the project plan and supporting documents
  - ☐ Project organization
  - ☐ Project team
  - ☐ Project metrics based on ROI
  - ☐ Purpose for new ERP

- [ ] Update the Project PERT/GANT Chart – high level to show timing for major steps, include cutover
- [ ] Approve the timing
- [ ] Present a time phased training program coordinated with the appropriate functionality rollout
- [ ] Phased rollout or big bang with justification for the decision
- [ ] Data conversion plan
- [ ] Plan to freeze non-critical activities on the current system
- [ ] Cost / Benefit Analysis with ROI
- [ ] Ask the tough questions
- [ ] Retain, replace or forego the use of an outside consultant

Review resources to move into implementation phase

- [ ] Is Top management still committed?
- [ ] Does the proposal cover what will happen if it is not accepted?
- [ ] Will the resources be available to execute the plan?
- [ ] Does the project have the right priority?
- [ ] Does the project have a budget?
- [ ] What are the restrictions?
- [ ] Is there a commitment to training?

Decision to proceed

- [ ] Reject
- [ ] Increase study granularity
- [ ] Scrap
- [ ] Take a different direction
- [ ] Executive Approval to Proceed
  - [ ] Team consensus
  - [ ] Executive champion approval
  - [ ] Steering committee approval
  - [ ] Executive staff approval
  - [ ] Board of Director approval
  - [ ] Go

Step 6 ERP Selection

With the project organization completed, ERP software selection carries the matching process down another level. The future state plan established the core systems specifications for the approved business case. In turn, these were broken down into software-related specifications and functionality, including the current and planned critical business needs.

For this step, sharply separate needs from wants. Regardless of the attractive options, focus on critical functionality. The analogy we use is of a beautiful car with a poor engine. While it looks great, it is not going to get you very far. The analogy continues. An operational car constructed of parts from a variety of spare cars may work, but one manufactured with a system of parts will be more efficient, last longer, and have more functionalities. Think about software as a system and not just as "chunks" of functionality. Middleware, whether it holds the software package together or integrates your applications into the system flow are never as efficient as fully integrated code. The middleware or "mashed" software products often introduce "gremlins," unexpected and difficult to fix glitches. Older SaaS applications were prone to this problem. Very carefully evaluate how each package is constructed.

Modular Systems

ERP systems are traditionally monolithic, with features and functions integrated into modules that are bundled into one package. The buyer gets full functionality in each module they purchase, regardless of need. Complete interchangeability and functionality selection like that provided by application software (apps) on an I-Pad, I-Phone, or Windows 8 are limited on most ERP software. While some software packages provide limited capability, in an ideal world, customers could pick specific apps and build their own version of a module.

Some packages offer scaled-down versions of the monolithic system, but embedded unused functionality is overhead. That has been the nature of the software business and for many reasons, it continues today.

You are, essentially, "married" to the selected software system, while paying for unusable functionality and dealing with greater implementation and operational complexity. Using another car analogy, if driving around town with one passenger, a small car will suffice. If fifty people are going across the country, take a bus. The point is not to pay for a bus when you need a small car.

The next illustration puts each MRP/ERP module into a discreet box and lists its functionality. The center block, "Requirements Planning – Foundations" is the ERP core connector, the engine. The blocks without stars are modules included in virtually all manufacturing packages. The five modules identified with a star are optional. Some, like MES, replace Shop Floor Control (SFC) and Production Activity Control (PAC) modules. Warehouse Management Systems (WMS), have greater application for distributors. CRM and Business Intelligence (BI) are expensive systems but are often platform independent. Content management supports Internet business processes. Its cousin, Document Management (not listed) is associated with document storage and retrieval.

Shop Floor Control (SFC)
- Labor reporting
- Material movement
- Work-in-process feedback
- Creation of Factory Paper
- Machine Utilization

Human Relations-Human Capital Management (HCM)
- Payroll
- Time and attendance
- Training
- Compliance with regulations
- Federal
- State

Supply Chain Management (SCM)
- Import/export management
- Product Visibility
- Customer information
- Product planning
- Logistics
- Track and Trace

Business Intelligence (BI)
- Analytics
- data warehousing
- data visualization (scorecards and dashboards)

Asset Management (EAM)
- Maintenance schedules
- Equipment performance
- Warranty management
- Hazardous material compliance
- Waste materials control
- Energy Management

Financial (ACCT)
- General Ledger
- Accounts Payable
- Accounts Receivable
- Project Accounting
- Budgeting
- Multi-operation

Customer Relationships (CRM)
- Relationship management
- Marketing analysis
- Inquiry by customer
- Order tracking
- Collaboration management
- Project management

Inventory Control (IC)
- Stock Status Control
- ABC Inventory Analysis
- Order Policy
- Inventory maintenance
- Physical Inventory
- Cycle counting
- Statistics

Operation Scheduling Production Activity Control (PAC)
- Dispatching sequence
- Order estimator
- Load summary by work center
- Priority Rules
- Queue Time Analysis
- Tool Control

- Pegged Requirements
- Full level
- Single level
- Multiple currencies
- Multiple plants / location
- Kitting

Manufacturing Execution (MES)
- Product and process definitions (PPM)
- Lifecycle management (PLM)
- Shop floor management
- Data collection
- Track and trace
- Performance analysis

Sales Forecasting (SFC)
- Model Selection
- Forecast Plans
- Evaluation and measurement

Purchasing
- Requisition and P.O. Preparation
- Purchase Order follow-up
- Purchase evaluation
- Vendor evaluation and selection

Requirements Planning - Foundation
- Finished production requirements – Gross to net
- Component requirements Gross to Net

Warehouse Management (WMS)
- Labor scheduling & management
- Complex picking process
- Forward pick logic
- Location management
- Preplanned put-a-way

Engineering Data Control
- Basic records file organization
- Engineering drawings
- Engineering changes
- Product Structure
- Standard routing
- Shop floor integration

Capacity Planning (CRP)
- Work center load report
- Planned order load
- Order start date calculations
- Load leveling

Order Processing
- Order management
- Available to promise
- Follow-up mechanisms
- Discounts
- Customer files

Content Management
- Documents
- Images
- Web-sites

The following illustration shows each module broken into five segments of proportional size. Numbered from one to five, segment size equates to functionality - the larger the number, the greater the functionality.

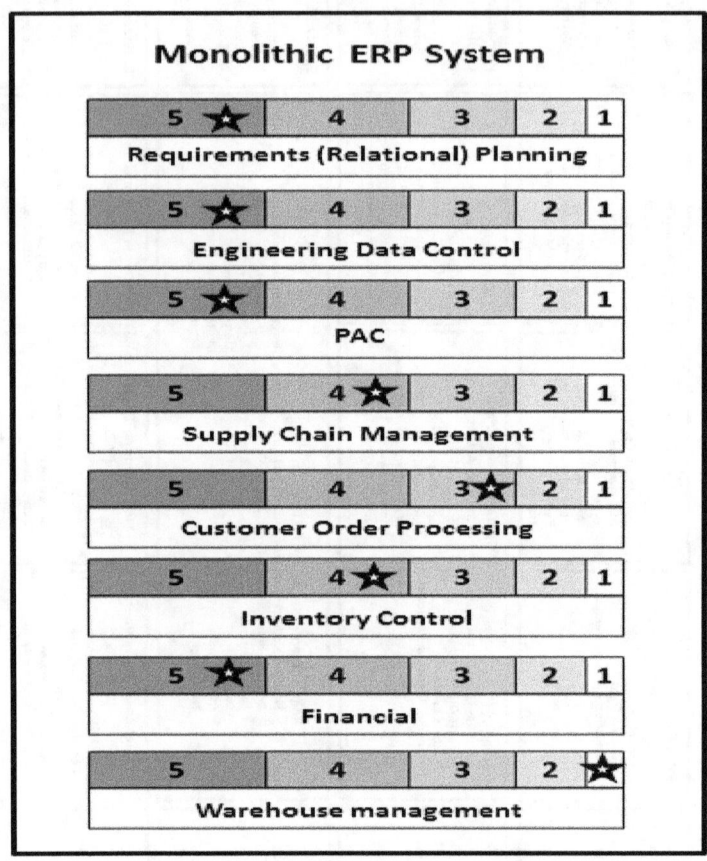

Illustration-Monolithic ERP System

The stars are used to quantity the functions needed by a complex, repetitive manufacturing company. This type of factory needs large segments for requirement's planning, engineering and PAC. In this example, the supply chain is a three, but most complex organizations have international supply chains. Order processing is straightforward, and a WMS is unnecessary. Inventory control rates a four, equaling the SCM requirement. Everyone wants a comprehensive financial system.

The point - when buying a package, the customer pays for "five" level functionality regardless of need. Purchasing expensive systems when a lower priced one is sufficient multiplies implementation cost and complexity. In the world of Lean Six Sigma, surpluses are a waste. One of the objectives is to find the right size system for your business.

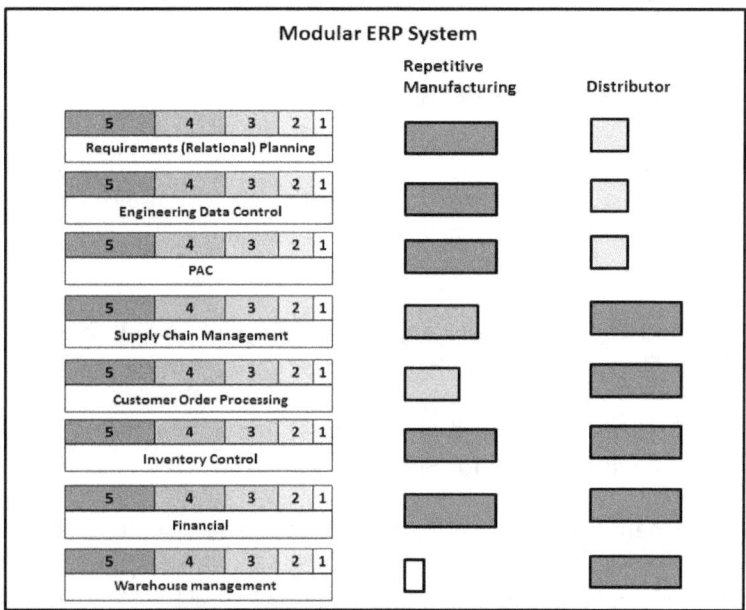

Illustration-Modular ERP System

The concept illustrated by this chart is the equivalent of disassembling a vehicle back into components of different size. Customers purchase systems components of the right size and pay for the associated functionality, no more and no less. In the second column, the same selection process applies to a distributor.

The shift towards app's friendly ERP has begun, but the majority of systems are monolithic. SaaS is evolving towards apps processing methodologies, but software design still lags manufacturing, where design has always involved both modularity and interchangeability.

Software Options

First-tier providers, Oracle, SAP, and Microsoft, serve the large, complex, multi-facility companies. They must also sell into the mid-market to survive. They offer scaled-down packages, with fewer features and functions to the small/medium sized (SMB) market. Functionality may be more than what tier two or three suppliers offer and make features and functions available in a competitive marketplace, but with a higher price tag.

Multiple features and functions are double-edged swords. With too many options, people attempt to use them all, and may not use any properly. The problem has a variation. Associates may not agree on which ones to use.

Tier two and three suppliers are, Epicor, Sage, Intuit, Infor, Lawson, Syspro, VAI, and many others, have rich and varied software products.

Most ERP customers fall within the small/medium sized range. This market is the battleground for ERP suppliers.

With the expansion of software into Application Service Providers (ASP), Service Oriented Applications (SOA), and SaaS, it is possible to have all the software and processing at a solution provider. This increases selection options while adding complexity to finding the right software solution.

The functionality variations between ERP systems run from minor to extreme. Any function can be different. There are critical distinctions and the selection team must understand what they need, and look beyond simple definitions to find exactly what the software does.

ERP solutions will always be as complex as the problems they must solve. The solution may look elegantly simple. In the end, you get what you pay for. What you save on software, may be lost with deficient capability, limiting flexibility.

Pareto Principle (80/20)

Some consulting and software companies apply the Pareto principle to ERP selection. While incorrectly attributed to Italian economist Vilfredo Pareto, Dr. Joseph M. Juran, used the principle to reinforce quality concepts.

He defined the Pareto principle as the vital few and the trivial many. In general, the principle states that focusing quality improvement on the top 20% of the issues will fix 80% of the problems. The principle has many applications, such as twenty percent of the SKU's generate eighty percent of the sales.

It helps to view The Pareto Principle from two perspectives, both insightful.

When matching business needs to ERP functionality, the team may agree that a certain percentage of matches, such as 80%, qualify a system for consideration. Implicit is the need to resolve the remaining 20% through workarounds, program modifications, or process changes.
The second part, the law of the trivial few, states that 20% of the issues are significant, and the rest are not. From this perspective, the company defines the thirty (arbitrary number) of critical applications and functionality. If the package provides these solutions, the other eighty percent are less necessary.

This concept has serious weaknesses, and teams need to rethink how to apply the 80/20 rule to ERP selection. Any package must pass a reasonability test and contain the required functionality. In the first example, one of the 80% can be the equivalent of a vital few in the second example. Critical functionality has priority in either event.

Eventually, apps will evolve, reducing the gap between software offered and needed, providing specific, focused functionality.

Functionality Check List

This functionality checklist is an updated version of the IBM "The Production Information Control System." It provides tracking for how much ERP has changed over the years, yet remains conceptually the same.

Core MRP/ERP

☐ Sales Forecasting
    ☐ Model selection
    ☐ Forecast plans
    ☐ Evaluation and measurement
    ☐ Sales and Operations Planning
    ☐ Advanced forecasting and budgeting

☐ Customer Order Processing
    ☐ Product configuration inquiry / matrix
    ☐ Corporate wide available to promise
    ☐ Unlimited line items
    ☐ On-line credit checking
    ☐ Easy customer and ship-to process
    ☐ Quotes
    ☐ Revision tracking
    ☐ Commission processing
    ☐ Sales analysis
    ☐ Drill down capabilities

☐ Engineering Data Control
    ☐ Basic records file organization
    ☐ Engineering drawings
    ☐ Engineering changes
    ☐ Product structure and standard routing records
    ☐ Full where used capabilities
    ☐ Interface with production equipment
    ☐ Maintenance processes for all engineering interfaces

- [ ] Inventory Control
  - [ ] Stock status control
  - [ ] ABC inventory analysis
  - [ ] Order policy
  - [ ] Inventory maintenance and update
  - [ ] Physical inventory
  - [ ] Multi-location for domestic and international
  - [ ] Available to promise
  - [ ] Allocation
  - [ ] Cycle counting
  - [ ] Location/lot tracking
  - [ ] Order/product tracking

- [ ] Requirements
  - [ ] Finished production requirements – gross to net
  - [ ] Component requirements gross to net
  - [ ] Special features
  - [ ] Kanban
  - [ ] Lot sizing
  - [ ] Offset requirements
  - [ ] Net change
  - [ ] Pegged requirements
    - [ ] *Full level*
    - [ ] *Single level*

- [ ] Purchasing
  - [ ] Requisition and PO preparation
  - [ ] Purchase order follow-up
  - [ ] Purchase evaluation
  - [ ] Vendor evaluation and selection

- [ ] Capacity Planning
  - [ ] Projected work center load report
  - [ ] Planned order load
  - [ ] Order start date calculations

- [ ] Load leveling
- [ ] Rough cut capacity planning
- [ ] Work center capacity planning

- [ ] Operation Scheduling
  - [ ] Dispatching sequence
  - [ ] Order estimator
  - [ ] Load summary by work center
  - [ ] Priority rules
  - [ ] Queue time analysis
  - [ ] Tool control
  - [ ] Kanban

- [ ] Shop Floor Control
  - [ ] Labor planning and reporting
  - [ ] Material movement
  - [ ] Work-in-process feedback
  - [ ] Creation of factory paper
  - [ ] Machine utilization
  - [ ] Tool planning
  - [ ] Special packaging
  - [ ] RFID
  - [ ] Bar Coding
  - [ ] Plan-o-Grams
  - [ ] Visual controls

Extended ERP

- [ ] Customer Relationship Management (CRM) – Marketing automation

- [ ] Sales Force Automation – (SFA) Customer support

- [ ] Product Lifecycle Management (PLM)
- [ ] Product Data Management (PDM)

- ☐ Supply-Chain Management (SCM)
  - ☐ Language
  - ☐ Customs
  - ☐ Management of FOB timing
  - ☐ In-transit tracking

- ☐ Warehouse management System
  - ☐ Multiple picking methods
  - ☐ Forward pick replenishment
  - ☐ Transportation Management

- ☐ Supply Chain collaboration (SCC)

- ☐ Field Service

- ☐ Financial Planning and Budgeting
  - ☐ Budgets
  - ☐ Simulations
  - ☐ Multiple charts of accounts
  - ☐ Currency conversion and management

- ☐ Manufacturing Execution Systems (MES)

- ☐ Document Management Systems
  - ☐ Content Management Systems

- ☐ Quality Management Systems

- ☐ Asset-Management Systems

- ☐ Multi-Plant processing

- ☐ Governance
  - ☐ Risk Compliance
  - ☐ Sustainability
  - ☐ Project Management

       ☐ Enterprise Performance Management (EPM)

☐ Intelligence Applications
       ☐ Business Intelligence (BI)
       ☐ Enterprise Manufacturing Intelligence (EMI)

☐ Energy Management

☐ Mobile technology

The Matching Process (Gap analysis)

☐ Use the future state as the basis for analysis
☐ Executive management has delegated the process to the team but must be closely involved
☐ Restate strategies into ERP features and functionality
☐ Map the current state gap analysis to strategy restatement
☐ Match type, style and model to global ERP suppliers and reduce list
☐ Match the capabilities and functions of the ERP package to the future state features and functions requirements

Analyze Potential ERP Suppliers

Each software provider offers a range of functionalities. Part of the section process is to construct a master list and grade each supplier on how well the functionality works for your company.

☐ Product demonstrations
☐ Site visits
☐ Finalize ERP supplier deliverables
☐ Supplier proposal
☐ Gap analysis field by field, file by file matching current ERP to new
☐ Boardroom review

The first task is to reduce the number of potential suppliers.

The objective is to match your organization to the large population of software suppliers and determine which potential providers fit the profile. It is important not to become obsessed with the largest provider in each category, nor to stay within a respective tier. Software systems are very diverse with considerable overlap in product functionality.

Based on the evaluation and your business shape, select the complexity that best defines your company.

Your Business Profile – Quantify					
Revenue	250m>	100-500m	25-250m	1-50m	0-5m
Number employees	2000>	1000>	50-1000	20-200	1-25
Number of users	60-1000>	30-1000	5-200	1-40	1-5
Data from: The Right Choice Makes All the Difference – http://softresources.com					
Product complexity	5	4	3	2	1
Process complexity	5	4	3	2	1
Multi-facility	5	4	3	2	1
Globalized	5	4	3	2	1
Spatial	5	4	3	2	1
Network complexity	5	4	3	2	1
Transactional volumes	5	4	3	2	1
Real Time	5	4	3	2	1
Five (5) = high One (1) =low					
Data from: Affinity Systems LLC					

Illustration-Your Business Profile

Match the following software tiers to your profile.

ERP Software Profile		
Level	**Type of software**	**Tier**
5 Highly complex	Enterprise	Tier One
4 Complex	Upper market	Tier One and Two
3 Medium Complex	Mid-market	Tier One, Two and Three
2 Somewhat Complex	Small to mid-market	Tier Two, Three and Four
1 Not complex	Small	Tier Five and/or SaaS

Illustration-ERP Software Profile

Select the associated price range. Note: there may be a SaaS solution available in any tier.

Software Price Range	
Tier One	750K to 2M
Tier Two	250K to 1.5M
Tier Three	25K to 250K
Tier Four	5K to 50K
Tier Five	$100 to $500

Data from: The Right Choice Makes All the Difference – http://softresources.com

Illustration-Software price range

Fill in the following summary.

Your software profile
Your complexity _____
Tiers applicable _____
Price range _____

Illustration-Your Software Profile

132

Observe the wide range of prices within and between each tier. The overlap in price is indicative of the overlap in functionality.

The objective is to get all needed functionality, with the least modifications, at the lowest price from a reliable, solvent, and viable supplier. There are, of course, other charges in addition to software price, including maintenance, user fees, etc., and due diligence will ferret them all out.

Following is a partial list of the software suppliers by tier.

Tier One
- SAP
- Oracle
- Microsoft

Tiers Two and three
- Infor/Lawson
- IFS
- MS Dynamics AX
- Oracle JD Edwards Enterprise One
- Sage
- Microsoft Dynamics Nav $ GP
- Sage 500 ERP
- Exact
- Exact Macola ES
- Infor 10 ERP Express
- SAP Business One
- Syspro
- NetSuite
- Epicor
- Consonal
- VAI
- Aviant

Many ERP software suppliers have acquired other companies and incorporated their products. In addition, they have developed fully integrated systems for different markets.

As in prior discussions, having all the software from one developer does not mean all the systems work together. They have multiple packages, developed using different languages, and protocols. Upgrading from one system to another is frequently tantamount to installing a new system from any supplier.

Use the following resources to help with your search.

> http://technologyevaluation.com/
> http://panorama-consulting.com/
> http://it.toolbox.com/
> http://softresources.com/

- ☐ Internet searches on software suppliers and products
- ☐ Professional publications
- ☐ Professional organizations
- ☐ Industry-specific chat rooms
- ☐ The use of search tools, such as those offered at TEC
- ☐ Using a consultant or consulting firm familiar with the industry, generalized ERP and industry-specific ERP packages

Reduce the number of potential suppliers to a manageable level. Use the strategic RFP to refine the match.

The Multi-Step RFP Process

Our research and studies have clearly determined the RFP is the most hated step in the process by both customer and supplier. Each software company surveyed felt significant changes were required in order to make it efficient.

Many respondents used the opportunity to lay the blame on consultants. Our research indicates no group occupies the moral high ground. It is important to recognize this can be the most wasteful, expensive and least value-adding step in the process.

The ERP supplier does not know if this is a potential client or someone doing a preliminary justification. Consequently, the salesperson rapidly fills in the answers to avoid automatically losing the sale. They may write, "A modification is required," when the requirement or solution is not readily apparent.

The process introduces ambiguity and error. You need a document that translates the strategic plan into ERP requirements, not a full features and functions list.

There are on line companies providing RFP services. Their capabilities range from poor to excellent. Visiting their websites and talking to ERP professionals will help you select the right candidates. Reliable services are not cheap, but they will work through the issues and send the RFP to the selected ERP suppliers and if requested, to others with which you are not familiar.

In order to shorten the time and increase the efficiency, approach the RFP like a Lean process and eliminate unnecessary steps. Break the process into smaller chunks focusing on the precise issues at each level. It makes little sense to get into the details of features of functions with suppliers without establishing higher-level requirements.

We suggest using a variation of the traditional RFP process.

Traditionally, customers prepare long detailed RFP's. ERP companies hate to fill them out. It takes a major time commitment to answer all the questions, and few internal people know enough to respond to all the complex issues.

At this point, in the process, six significant sets of documentation are available if the due diligence was correctly completed.

- [ ] Strategy statements reshaped into software terms
- [ ] Future State plans
- [ ] Project Plan
- [ ] Process designs for the top 30 issues
- [ ] Preliminary schedule
- [ ] Technology integration plan

Strategic RFP

The Strategic RFP (also called a mini-RFP) communicates the core business requirements.

- Take the unnecessary work (waste) out of the RFP process
- Make your proposal viable to the ERP suppliers
- Provide the relevant information
- Avoid unnecessary responses to long, complicated preliminary RFP
- Increase the quality of responses from the suppliers

Following is a check-off list for a mini-RFP.

- [ ] Name
- [ ] Description of the company
- [ ] SKU (Item Master Key) field size
- [ ] Number of plants and types
- [ ] Products/services produced/offered at each facility
- [ ] Size of company – use a relative scale if can't give out the information
- [ ] Organization
- [ ] Hardware, software and network configuration
- [ ] Existing database structures
- [ ] Key dates
- [ ] Submission requirements and cutoff dates
- [ ] Response format, hardcopy, e-mail or CD
- [ ] Transaction volumes

- ☐ Two-page strategy statement translated into ERP terms
- ☐ Thirty key operational requirements - informational/and or process designs (may want to hold for features and functions RFP)
- ☐ Electronic Data Interchange (EDI) requirements- who supplies and how?
- ☐ Type of company (make a check-off matrix)
- ☐ Multi-plant / multi-company
- ☐ Integrated accounting with logic for Sarbanes-Oxley
- ☐ Industry type; ETO, BTO, ATO, or process manufacturing
- ☐ Supply-chain management with automobile industry
- ☐ Supply chain with multi-language and country processing capability
- ☐ Names of countries in the supply chain
- ☐ Engineering interfaces
- ☐ Inventory location management in multiple locations
- ☐ Support a visual system
- ☐ Supports Lean principles
- ☐ Picking logic for wave, less than case pack, bin locations and auto replenishment of forward, less than case pack picking locations
- ☐ Support's radio frequency (RFID)
- ☐ Support's bar coding
- ☐ Plan-O-Grams
- ☐ Customer shipping requirements
- ☐ It supports mobile technology
- ☐ Include cloud requirements

Send the strategic RFP to a number of ERP suppliers in all categories.

- ☐ Traditional ERP suppliers
- ☐ SaaS
- ☐ Best of breed, or industry-specific software companies

When provided with these are high-level requirements, suppliers will appropriately evaluate the strategic RFP.

Telephone interviews

Reduce the list to five before sending out a features and functions RFP. There are several ways to accomplish this:

- ☐ Telephone interviews
- ☐ Online demos
- ☐ Online chat rooms
- ☐ Online ERP evaluation web sites
- ☐ ERP company web site

Features and Functions Request for Proposal (RFP)

The features and functions RFP is synonymous with the traditional RFP proposal. It must be in sufficient detail and focused on the top 20 or 30 most important criteria. The RFP must represent all the associates, who must agree that all central issues and criteria are sufficiently covered. Send the RFP/RFQ to the survivors of the strategic RFP process.

The focus can now shift to the features and functions. Suppliers have qualified by filling out and submitting a strategic RFP. It does not make any sense to repeat information. It should come back in a summarized form through the deliverables, spell out the evaluation criteria, and restate the key dates.

Set priorities and assign weights to features and function's selection criteria. If a Selection Service is used you may want to do simulations with different weights.

Get steering committee approval on the selection criteria before issuing the RFP. This reduces questions about the selection process.

Suppliers will ask who their competitors are. There are different schools of thought about how to answer this question. One side feels that knowing provides an incentive to prepare more thoroughly. Other companies will not divulge competitors because two negative effects may occur. Suppliers use the information to compare their system favorably to their competitors and this frequently includes product bashing at the demo. You want the supplier to concentrate on their ERP system and how it solves your business issues. Vendors may feel they have a built-in disadvantage and drop out of the race. While troubling it aids in the reduction process. Draw your own conclusion about how to handle the question.

The RFP should:

- ☐ Support the mission and strategies, not the glitz
    - ☐ Account information needs
    - ☐ Flow within the business

- ☐ Key field sizes
    - ☐ Item master
    - ☐ Description
    - ☐ Group technology number
    - ☐ Product structure
    - ☐ Multiple representations, e.g. SKU for multiple customers

- ☐ Features and functions:
    - ☐ Non-technology related
    - ☐ Solution Oriented

- ☐ It describes each business function:
    - ☐ In detail
    - ☐ Relationship between them
    - ☐ Process designs if not submitted as part of the strategic RFP

- ☐ Need to consider:
    - ☐ Cost – (insufficient scope and detail)
    - ☐ Solution support needs
    - ☐ Life cycle solutions
    - ☐ Ongoing charges

- Total cost of ownership
- The effects of increased velocity (throughput) on asset management
- Scalability
- Frequency and method of ERP updates
  - Batch
  - Real-time
  - Capability to selectively perform both

- Address all facets of the solution
  - Project schedule
  - Iterative or big-bang implementation methodology
  - Database
  - Applications
  - Network
  - Security
  - Hardware
  - Vendor support
  - Education
  - Implementation time line
  - Modifications (need slide for modifications)
  - Detail "supported/not supported"

Responses will become an addendum to the contract.

There is an option to the features and functions RFP titled "ERP Company Deliverables." After evaluating packages, ask the suppliers to submit the deliverable's document. If they reject the RFP, but you like the product, they should not object to a document spelling out the deliverables in enough detail to establish accountability. If they refuse to provide this document, switch on the caution lights. If the supplier remains on your list, pursue other options establishing legal accountability, such as a super detailed contract showing all the deliverables.

The danger to the ERP supplier using the deliverable process instead of the features and functions may be the lack of detail on specifics. This puts them at a disadvantage for evaluation and you at a disadvantage if deliverables fail to meet expectations.

By not following the RFP format, some suppliers make it difficult to compare packages. If obtaining the information through the RFP, follow-up with the vendor before the evaluation is completed. If derived from the deliverable, there is not an obligation to achieve parity. If suppliers fail to provide the appropriate competitive information, it is their problem, not yours. If you feel responsible for giving suppliers the opportunity to answer iterative questions, perhaps the RFP was insufficient or the needs were unclear. Get the answer and include it in the deliverables. Know what you want because iterations cost money and time. Include the following minimal deliverables.

- [ ] Specifically state how it satisfies the strategic requirements
- [ ] Specifically address the 30 key issues
- [ ] Specifically define how the gap issues will be solved (solutions to the business problems not sufficiently resolved by the features and functions of the package). This could be modifications, work a rounds or manual processes (including PC's)
- [ ] How many and what types of modifications are required, how much they will cost, and when will they be done
- [ ] Software supplier team assignment
- [ ] Document how to measure performance
- [ ] Completion date
- [ ] All costs broken down by type
- [ ] Projected schedule of expenses

Analyze Responses to the RFP's

One technique is to use a white board and layout a spreadsheet of the core requirements with a column for each ERP supplier. Grade the functionality of each with a score of 0-5.

5 = Better than required
4 = Meets all requirements
3 = Meets minimal requirements – some work around needed
2 = Questionable – some modifications required
1= Significant modifications required
0 = Not available

Prepare the metric either visually or on-line. The responses to the RFP will provide a rough-cut look at the criteria. Each team member will fill out the scorecard immediately after any demo or site visit.

Go through each of the thirty key criteria and assign a weighted value. Multiply the weight of the feature/function rank to calculate the score.

Update your board and/or Excel program.

Update the parking lot list.

Leave room for comments. If the core functionality issues do not get a high score, reject the product. If you are uncertain about how to score or what a company meant with a certain response, call them. If they are near to you, ask them to stop by. This is not a demo. It is fact gathering. Score keeping is not a game. You are searching for the truth.

There is debate about which should come first, the site visit or the demo. Although the site visit can help reduce the number of suppliers on the list, it is time-consuming and expensive. The demo will provide the team with the knowledge needed to evaluate the ERP package. Save the site visits for the final selection process.

Call Current Customers

The vendor's customer list will provide insight into what type of companies use the software. Call the contacts list to see how they feel about the ERP and product usability. Make sure the ERP matches the core requirements. If the clients are manufacturing running ERP/ MRP Systems, and you are a distributor, proceed with caution.

Vendor Analysis

Get financial data and thoroughly check out the suppliers. Make sure they are profitable and will remain viable. Find out their history on updates and ease of use. If they cannot pass these qualifying steps, do not invite them to demo.

Many ERP suppliers are private companies, and not required to make their financial data public, and therefore, are reluctant to share it. Inform them that proof of financial viability is required before getting the order. They may wait until the executive visit to share it (given the need for a visit). If they choose not to divulge the information, you are not obligated to keep them on the list. You are the customer, and entitled to the affirmation needed for fulfillment of due diligence.

Cut the List

At this point, the project team has the knowledge to reduce competition to two or three suppliers. The team must reach a consensus, and then meet with the executive champion and steering committee. All must agree before proceeding.

After gaining team consensus, contact the suppliers to ensure their continued interest. We consider the definition of consensus as "I can live with the decision, support it, and make the system work."

Put together a demo schedule. Since everyone will want to present last, there are several ways to determine the priority. One is to draw names. A second way is to poll the team. It may seem arbitrary and less fair, but fairness is not the issue. You are trying to get the right ERP for your business. Schedule the demo sequence your team wants, without any apologies.

Demo – Potential Combat Zone

Demos are a problem for ERP suppliers. They must somehow summarize your business data into a structure allowing the demo of all your business conditions. They normally have an accumulation of customer data in their computers. Remember, they are demonstrating a capability so be patient and open-minded but cautious.

One sign of commitment is when they visit up to one week before the demo, tour the business, interview associates, and perform their own evaluation, then integrate your company data into their system. If they are not willing to take this critical step, remove them from your list and move along. A demo without your data is just another show and tell.

In today's complex ERP environment, many companies are forgoing this step and focusing on the core functionality with product designs from the future state. The decision on which approach to take depends on the complexity of the organization and software, the level of knowledge in the enterprise, the existence of legacy system, and the size of the project. Regardless, the supplier should be able to demo the functionality for the top thirty issues or provide enough real evidence that it exists and meets the documented requirements.

Bypassing the demo puts extreme pressure on obtaining the appropriate documentation and inclusion of the software deliverables in the contract.

Given this exception in the evolution of ERP, many companies will and should insist on demonstrations. Smaller companies often buy tier 3 or 4 software packages and at this level, the suppliers are less solvent and buyers may wind up with orphan systems.

Establish and communicate the basis for scoring. Make sure they understand you will grade the demonstration on the live system only, and Power Point presentations or "future functionality" receives zeros.

Demos are fascinating affairs. Some presenters are brutally honest; others oversell functionality and some lie. The ERP software industry is a tough, highly competitive business. Accept that fact and prepare to deal with it. If they try to lie, or misrepresent the product, and you know it, nail them to the wall. Be prepared for a dog and pony show but make presenters stick to your requirements. Some vendors want to focus on sophisticated and highly desirable functions that differentiate their product. First, make sure they satisfy all core issues, those on the closed-loop chart, and your top thirty issues. In general, ERP representatives cannot afford a failure. It hurts their sales effort at other accounts and can be expensive to rectify. They must also live up to the conditions in the contract. Questions about functionality are the reason to include RFP documents and deliverables in the contract.

Make a distinction between technical support and the salesperson. The technical person has no incentive to misstate functionality because if assigned to the project they have to make the system work. There are still no excuses. Uncover their agenda by asking whether they will be a part of the implementation team. If not, are they part of the sales support team? If yes, be wary.

Do:

- Look for the truth. Just because they say it, does not make it true or false. In the final analysis, only the facts are important.
- No glitz, stick to the core issues until understood.
- Start a parking lot list of unresolved issues and make sure they answer all the issues and concerns before signing a contract.
- Ask questions – it is not the time to be shy. We have seen far too many cases where members of the user community were afraid to ask good questions even when they needed answers. Project Leaders and executive champions, encourage your team to ask the tough questions, and do not hold it against them.
- Cover all-important issues.
- Remember, team members will have to live with the results – perhaps for a long time.
- Make sure they use your data in the presentation.
- If you cannot break the code, it is not real.
- Ask pointed, tough questions.
- Update the parking lot list.

Question:

- ☐ Is functionality equal to or better than the requirement?
- ☐ Is the system scalable?
- ☐ Is the system easy to use? If yes, prove it.
- ☐ Does the system function as advertised?
- ☐ Are they willing to put the RFP into the contract without change?
- ☐ Are they willing to submit a set of deliverables?
- ☐ Can you work with them?
- ☐ Does the system fulfill the requirements on the list?
- ☐ Does the system support the strategies?
- ☐ Were business critical functionality properly demonstrated?
- ☐ Does the system support real-time processing?
- ☐ Does the system support mobile communications technology?

If the software supplier uses a demo program or PowerPoint, it defeats the purpose. Ask or observe if the code is real, if not, mark zero on your evaluation for all functions covered in this way.

If a given functionality is in development or listed as future enhancements, ignore them for evaluation purposes. A tested enhancement or added functionality may be weeks or years in the future. The truth is you do not know, and if you did, the data to match it to your needs will not be available. If they do not have it now, score a zero, but other suppliers may not offer it either, so flag it for future consideration.

How willing are they to make modifications, and at what cost?

Parking lot lists, Modifications and Middleware

Few systems will offer all the needed functions. Post the gap issues on a parking lot list at the start of the selection process and update it at every step. It is worth the price and space to devote one large marking board in the war room for problem visualization. Discuss and document proposed solutions and frequently visit progress on defining the solutions. Modifications become especially contentious when they are

146

difficult and/or take a long time to program and implement. Constantly check if the vital 30 are covered.

Match your activities plan to the parking lot list. Make sure nothing falls through the cracks. It is important to resolve all issues before signing the contract. In the heat of an implementation, getting key functions resolved and solutions implemented becomes difficult. The result is often a compromise forcing awkward and expensive work-a-rounds and/or extensive development costs. In addition, it also causes missed due dates.

One purpose for a parking lot list is isolating non-supported functional requirements. Executive management needs to keep a sharp eye on this activity. Converting the list into ERP modification proposals generates expense and time-consuming modifications. Worse, the ERP supplier may not provide ongoing support, and you will incur additional, ongoing expenses installing upgrades or future modifications.

Program Modifications

Modifications (mods) are one of the more serious issues in the selection process, as they are expensive, time-consuming and require perpetual technical support. When the parent software is updated or upgraded, it may dictate costly changes to the modification or middleware. One of the key questions is how to maintain the modification, and at what cost, given future updates.

During the software investigation and the demo, the ERP supplier must help identify the mismatches between your requirements and the software capabilities. If functionality is lacking or extensive modifications required, they must address the issue honestly or take a chance the truth will eventually eliminate their product. You have to decide if there is value in continuing to look at the system. Given correct information, clients tend to make the right decision.

Installing ERP systems improves productivity, but only when a process is changed for the better. Changing processes often complicates some work and reduces efficiency. The user community will point out these situations, but it only counts when someone listens. It is easy to dismiss complaints as "not adjusting" to change. Increasing the difficulty in one part of the system will increase the efficiency in the rest. Communicate tradeoffs to the user community. If they understand the need, they will help implement the change.

Suppliers are not going to make a major investment for a specific solution. They might combine your requirements with those from other clients to produce a marketable product, and the process may extend the implementation while the result may be an imprecise solution. These are enhancements, not modifications, and they can put the project in jeopardy, escalate the cost, and dramatically increase the risk of failure. Software development takes time, and the effect ripples through the project. Customers are not in the development business, and for them, it is a non-value added activity. When you see this situation unfolding, modify your contract to maximize your investment.

An option might be for the supplier to collaborate with and integrate third-party software. The solution may involve writing a middleware interface. Evaluate and calculate the benefits and disadvantages of each approach.

There are numerous stories about software developers who ignore the user community when drawing up the specs for a modification. Software programmers often think they have better solutions than users. Failure to listen to the voice of the user causes failure in all the previous categories. Do not let this happen on your project. This note of caution extends to management, consultants, supplier, and project management.

Once the modification is completed, the software may fail to perform the task exactly as required. One major cause is the failure to involve the user community in the definition. This is an egregious action.

The timing for the completion is seldom precise and may affect training schedules. Since learning is a building-block process, lack of training in one module will make some downstream training incomplete. The scheduled completion for modifications is often well into the project, causing a chain reaction. Projects are time phased, and events scheduled in sequence. The hardware schedule may be firm, and equipment may have to wait for the modification.

Software Development Process

It took forty years for the software-development cycle to mature. There is no excuse for ignoring it. The magnitude of the change and morphing into an enhancement will become clear in the process. Without resorting to any technical jargon, the iterative development cycle is:

1. User specification – A programmer, systems analyst, or consultant meets with the associates and documents the requirement. This includes all inputs, processes, outputs, volumes, who, what, how and why it is done, why is it important, when it is used and where it applies. Define and document potential solutions.

2. Conceptual design - A plan, flow charts, and specifications list describing how the redesigned system will work. This is an iterative process involving the user community, consultant and software developer. The user must drive the definition and agree to the solution. Develop an action plan using checklists for each step. Define test scripts. Prepare three estimates: completion date, hours, and cost.

3. Approval process - Associates approve detail changes because they affect how the formulas will function and how the product will work. The user community and project manager must approve all changes to the detail design.

4. The detail design uses the customer specification and the conceptual design to develop program specifics. Frequently, the detail design causes changes in the conceptual design. The user

149

community must be involved in resolving all detail issues. Update the three estimates and document the reason for missed dates.

5. The programming conventions and methodologies used by the supplier, such as language, are transparent. The client needs assurance the design will work, be on time, within budget, and of high quality. The user community must have test scripts prepared by this time. Prepare and distribute project updates: on time or late to schedule and variance to budgeted dollars and hours.

6. Structure the test with associates – use a test database.

7. Test process - The developer will run a number of tests to debug a program before turning it over to the client for review. In reality, they cannot test all possible conditions. Testing is an iterative process involving the user and developer.

8. Document the modification in two forms. Include programming, systems, and user instructions. Specifications for user approval, regardless of programming protocols, must be clear, relevant, and easy to read. Forcing an iterative development process assures that needed documentation will be available.

9. Fix all issues as they occur - Testing may reveal problems in the programming or the design. Heavy workloads and late project performance will create a temptation to avoid the additional work. Saying the system is good enough is not acceptable. Make sure it is a quality application. People will be living with the result for a long time, and flaws creating inefficiencies have long-term effects. The cost to fix it later will increase total cost. This is where the Lean mentality is useful – do it right the first time.

10. The supplier and user community must update the documentation, and the supplier provides written documentation stating the program tested successfully, and no further work is required. It still has to pass the full systems test. Update the three estimates with

real data, showing the variance to the plan and actual performance. In some cases, this is an invoice.

11. Use the documentation and real data to test the modification. Sign off only after the modification has satisfied all the requirements and the user community and project manager accept the modification.

It is expensive to develop or modify software regardless of where it resides. SaaS systems modification's costs may be equal or greater than on-premise, if the provider even allows modifications. Where the software does not fit the business processes, a decision is required, "Do we change the process or modify the software?" Gather the evidence from internal sources and the software supplier before answering the question. Bake the evidence and the decision into the deliverables and the contract.

Site Visits

Site visits are costly, taking project members away from the business. Save them until the finalists are determined. Arrange visits to companies with similar business profiles.

- Relational (product complexity)
- Process complexity
- Multi-facility
- Network complexity
- Spatial
- Transactional
- Real-time

Note that similar products are not criteria. Competitors are normally reluctant to share what could be sensitive information.

An ERP supplier unable to find parallel clients within your vertical may not have experience with your business type.

Make sure the walk meets the talk. Take notes and use the selection criteria defined for the evaluation. The goal of the team may be the same, but members gain different perspectives and make individual observations. Have team members immediately fill out evaluations.

Include the aforementioned forms and notes about the ERP system applicability to your organization, observations raising flags and other relevant information. Immediately update the scoreboard.

Selection

By this time, the team not only has the information required to make a decision but also is probably tired of the investigation. It is important for the team leader to keep them focused and not rush to judgment.

The team must reach consensus on the winner and runner up. The result must have the functionality to support all associates or find a different package.

Select two finalists because the process can still break down in negotiation. A split decision between office functionality and operations should favor operations. If the ERP system does not work for production, distribution, and supply chain management, no one will be happy.

Share the decision with the steering committee. If they concur with the choice, notify the top two suppliers of their status.

Executive Visit to ERP Company

The executive visit to the supplier company is a critical step.

The steering committee and the team need to work with the executive to prepare for the visit. The project team must provide an issue list, including the contents of the parking lot list. The executive team must obtain answers for each critical issue.

☐   Document issues

152

- [ ] Have legal and finance review the proposal
- [ ] Meet with the project team, including the consultant
- [ ] Consider taking a financial member of the project team
- [ ] Understand all issues on the parking lot list and their proposed solution
- [ ] Review the billing structure
- [ ] Discuss timing and penalty for late install
- [ ] Discuss composition of the vendor project team and process for replacing incompatible personnel
- [ ] Make it clear what expenses will and will not be reimbursed
- [ ] Discuss other mutual opportunities, such as shared revenue for the development of an enhancement

Use the opportunity to compare company values and establish relationships with the executive personnel. The visit will determine the partnership potential and the degree of transparently. The result needs to be high-level commitment on both sides.

To this point, it is useful to discuss important common interests.

Discuss metrics and accountability and make sure suppliers understand that all contracts must have detail backup behind the proposals, and all will receive a final legal review. Get the RFP/ letter of deliverables if not supplied to the project team. Make sure you discuss it openly and thoroughly, and most importantly, do not reach a legal agreement without a detailed commitment included in the contract.

If the ERP supplier has not provided financial information, ask for it now. If the supplier is not forthcoming, visit the runner-up to see if they are a viable supplier.

Final Decision

Following the visit(s), the executive group meets with the project team, exchanging information and finalizes the decisions.

Notify the first place supplier, establish a date, and time for final contract negotiations. Ask again for any outstanding documents or deliverables.

Contract

The responsibility for contract negotiations and approval belongs to executive management. While the project team provides valuable inputs, successful contracts are the result of practiced negotiators. Approval by the Board of Directors is highly recommended.

Cloud computing decisions involve software, hardware, and personnel in a mix of on-premise and off premise computing. Make sure the team has at least one member who understands this methodology.

The Executive Champion often conducts the negotiations. They should include other key personnel.

- ☐ Project Leader
- ☐ Consultant
- ☐ Someone who understands contracts (e.g. – CFO)
- ☐ Someone who understands Information Technology (e.g.-CIO)

The person or team conducting the negotiations needs the following:

- ☐ Complete understanding of solution needs
- ☐ Technical knowledge or accompanied by someone with it
- ☐ Familiar with ERP negotiations (e.g. modifications, missed dates)
- ☐ Incorporate supplier proposals into the contract including deliverables and all forms of the RFP
- ☐ Do a future state run-through with the project team and executive steering committee to ensure all needed functionalities are in the contract
- ☐ Make sure it has a thorough legal review

The contract must cover all these points at a minimum:

- [ ] Software
- [ ] Maintenance
- [ ] Number of users
- [ ] Per user fees
- [ ] Upgrades
- [ ] Additional modules (lock in future)
- [ ] Consulting fees by classification
- [ ] Software company billing procedure
- [ ] Hourly consulting rates
- [ ] Estimate of the total cost
- [ ] Expenses by category
- [ ] Application modifications
- [ ] Training – spell out who, when, end associates and technical personnel
- [ ] Train the trainer or train the company
- [ ] Training method – on the site, via video conference
- [ ] Maintenance fees and when they start
- [ ] By whom and at what cost
- [ ] What are the cost savings opportunities for co-development
- [ ] Compare costs for Big-Bang vs. Phased implementation
- [ ] Make sure the conversion methodology is clear
- [ ] Negotiate percent hold back until the system functions as promised
- [ ] Ability to change incompatible supplier team members
- [ ] Hardware and other equipment supplied by software provider
- [ ] Time phased expenditure plan
- [ ] Spell out Disaster-Recovery Plans
- [ ] Backup
- [ ] Restore
- [ ] Documentation
- [ ] Change management process
- [ ] Technical services
- [ ] Deliverables
- [ ] Addendums where required

ERP Company Deliverables

The company buying the ERP system needs an agreement of deliverables, including but not limited to costs, and the projected completion date.

- ☐ The contract has proposals meeting strategic requirements
- ☐ Specific solutions to the 30 key operational issues
- ☐ Solutions to the open issues, including the parking lot list
- ☐ How many and what types of modifications are required, how much they will cost and when will they be done
- ☐ Penalties for late modifications
- ☐ The persons assigned from the supplier
- ☐ Performance metrics
- ☐ Project Justification, Cost/Benefit Analysis and ROI
- ☐ On-premise or Cloud solutions or a hybrid

If you do not like the way negotiations are preceding, terminate the process. If issues cannot be resolved at this level, before the sale is complete, they will be extremely difficult to solve after signing the contract. Changes are nearly impossible once the project is in process.

Sign the Contract

- ☐ Legal review
- ☐ Executive approval
- ☐ Now it is time for action
- ☐ Sign the contract

Map Legacy Systems to New System

With the contract signed, technical personnel from the software suppliers will meet with your internal information technology experts. Make sure everyone is qualified to perform this very important process. They must map the current system to the selected system in detail, field to field, and define what actions are required to convert from the legacy system to the new one. The team of experts defines the data conversion methodology and identifies the resources needed to achieve it. Some conversion options are:

- ☐ Programmatic – must write and debug programs.
- ☐ Data entry –trained entry personnel must be available.

Information technology personnel from both sides perform this step. It does not replace the boardroom review.

Note: Some companies prefer to conduct the Business Simulation or Boardroom Pilot, defined in Chapter 7, at this point in the sequence.

Implementation Project Plan

The project manager, lead consultant from the Software Company, and independent consultant must update the project plan with details and time lines. The relationship between events is critical. Updating the PERT or a Gant Chart will establish proper time sequences. The project manager is responsible for this activity.

Establish the dates for a beginning physical inventory or comprehensive cycle count to initiate the system. This is a joint financial and inventory management decision.

Establish implementation dates based on the rhythms of the business cycles. If, for example, September is the busiest month, and January is the slowest month, then January is a better "go live" date.

- ☐ Plan project completion dates for the last weekend of the month, to accommodate end of month accounting cutoffs. This provides the time to pull old paperwork and replace it with new, or validate electronic images.
- ☐ Identify all action items (need team input to complete assignments)
- ☐ Prepare/update project PERT/GANT chart
- ☐ Physical inventory/cycle count date
- ☐ Project matrix

☐ Make sure there is a contingency plan if the system fails

It is the Project Leader and consultants' responsibility to get commitments from the team, prioritize, and apply finish dates to the action items.

☐ Plan training to coincide with implementation schedule
☐ Action items- completion dates may realistically change:
  ☐ Tasks to be completed
  ☐ Expected duration
  ☐ Planned completion date
  ☐ Assigned responsibility
  ☐ Consequences of being late (relational implications)
  ☐ Signoff
☐ Develop a process methodology for data purification, conversion, and migration
  o Manual
  o Automated
  o Who will manage/control
☐ Progress measurements Develop progress measurements and KPI's
☐ Develop reporting methodology and implement it
☐ Define and Implement change control procedures
☐ Review final plans
☐ Discuss any date changes
☐ Finalize commitments
☐ Finalize resources
☐ Finalize priorities
☐ Team sign-off on the plan

Update the Executive Steering Committee

☐ Approval to proceed
☐ Post copies to an intranet

Prepare the Organization

- [ ] The project team meets with the executive staff and reviews the plan, benefits and ROI
- [ ] Plan is go, no go or return to the drawing board

Project Kickoff Meeting

Bring all the members up to date on the project. Meet with the entire organization in one group or a series of meetings. Normally, someone will ask if the project is going to result in layoffs or outsourcing of jobs. The executive staff must have an answer.

- [ ] Emphases the importance of the program to the future of the company - its ability to compete grows.
- [ ] Ask for everyone's help and commitment.
- [ ] Communicate the program: how it will work, what the process will be, what the expectations are the metrics.
- [ ] Announce who will be on the project team and their roles.
- [ ] Explain how their jobs will be backfilled or handled.
- [ ] Emphasis the project team will need support from all associates and top management.
- [ ] Establish communications and the project parameters.
- [ ] Emphasis to all associates the importance of keeping task commitments and maintaining high-quality standards, while maintaining all critical routine business processes.
- [ ] Reiterate consequences for missed dates.
- [ ] Explain tracking mechanism: Intranet, bulletin boards, or internal newsletter.
- [ ] Spell out the training expectations relative to module, and mandatory attendance at sessions.
- [ ] Spell out communications loops.
- [ ] Planned completion dates.
- [ ] Establish a grievance process.

Now it is time to get the job done - right!

Step 7 Implementation

In our experience, individual implementation plans are variable but the overall steps are generic. The enterprise has agreed on the following, starting with the Implementation Project Plan covered in the previous chapter.

Approval to Go

- ☐ Purpose of the new ERP
- ☐ Cost/benefit analysis
- ☐ Implementation schedule
- ☐ Selection rationale
- ☐ Team consensus
- ☐ Executive Champion approval
- ☐ Steering Committee approval
- ☐ Executive Staff approval
- ☐ Board of Director approval

Document of Understanding

- [ ] Product components to life cycle – the business understands needed changes and the actions required to achieve it.
- [ ] Personnel to support the implementation – team members at all levels have their assignments. Technical and end associates – there is sufficient support personnel to take care of the specific issues and there are persons on the team with knowledge of the processes.
- [ ] Internal support - team members understand their support roles and managers incorporate everyone into functional teams.
- [ ] Preliminary costs are documented and reflected in the budget.
- [ ] Current applications are documented and understood.
- [ ] Everyone has completed some level of training on ERP.

Business Simulation or Boardroom Pilot

This step, regardless of label, is critical in the process. In summary, the company sets aside several days, for the ERP supplier and the associates, to detail match the new ERP system to the current system. The objective is to introduce the ERP team, teach the system to the associates, match functionalities, resolve mismatches, establish priorities and schedules, resolve conflicts between the systems and to communicate the plan and expectations. Associates prepare scripts from actual documents and processes in advance of the meeting.

On some projects, this step occurs immediately after mapping the old to the new system, and prior to detail assignment. The project manager and software leader will establish where to fit the process into the proper sequence. Like the Future State, some companies bypass this step. This is a critical process error. Do it and do it right.

Highlight the unresolved issues on the parking lot list. This may be the last opportunity to resolve them without contention.

The first requirement is normally to set up systems codes, frequently done in the Business simulation and requiring precision. These are the premises for information processing, and they determine how business activities interact between modules. Carefully document all systems codes and their functions, for use in troubleshooting improper data processing or results.

The process is generic.

- ☐ Familiarize associates with the system
    - ☐ Features
    - ☐ Functions
    - ☐ Modules
- ☐ Environment review
    - ☐ User
    - ☐ Database
    - ☐ Tools
    - ☐ Security
    - ☐ Technology
- ☐ Outline and establish the training process
    - ☐ Relationship of training to implementation
    - ☐ How training will be done to accommodate modifications
    - ☐ Who will be trained
    - ☐ How they will be trained: train the trainer or "everyone"
    - ☐ Executive as well as associates
- ☐ Resolve issues such as
    - ☐ Multiple plants
    - ☐ Timing
    - ☐ How they are tied together
    - ☐ Corporate and individual database architecture
    - ☐ Equipment differences
- ☐ Systems codes of all types – setup
    - ☐ This includes chart of accounts
    - ☐ Identify contents
    - ☐ Reach approval
- ☐ Load the systems codes and help determine if the interaction of the codes creates conflicts.

- ☐ Load the test scripts for the complete order / production / billing cycle and end of month financial closing.
- ☐ Analyze all outputs and compare the two systems. Document and resolve all deviations.
- ☐ Resolution of all parking lot issues discovered during the boardroom test and subsequent discussions.
- ☐ Final definition of all work-a-rounds, process changes, modifications and middle ware.
- ☐ Review and resolve any conflicts with critical success factors.

Once the project starts, force a decision on the legacy system. At some point, it becomes undesirable and non-productive to fix or maintain the old system. Force all legacy systems changes through the steering committee with a signoff by the executive champion. Shift the resources to the new system.

Summary of Implementation Steps

- ☐ Project plan
- ☐ Major milestones
- ☐ Tasks to be completed
- ☐ Expected duration
- ☐ End dates
- ☐ Person responsible
- ☐ Consequences of being late
- ☐ Sign-offs
- ☐ Progress measurements by responsibility and project
- ☐ Use change control procedures

Conversion Databases

- ☐ Establish appropriate data bases - may be an integral part of the package
  - ☐ A sandbox is a database where associates can play without concern for data or test integrity.

163

- Testing – A database where associates can test their processes and no one can change the data without coordinating with others.
- Go live – where corrected or converted files are stored.
- Start the data conversion plan as soon as possible.

Stick to Plan – Execution

- Stick to plan
- Implement production systems and information systems changes in parallel
- Coordinate process and software changes – special concern - modifications
- Make sure people are accountable for on time completion
- Update PERT/GANT charts and other visual documentation as action items are completed
- Find out what problems are preventing action
- Solve problems rapidly to prevent ripples of delay
- Check off completed events and tasks
- Implement change control
- Get user involvement on all data changes such as descriptions and codes
- Determine who has access to the supplier hotline
- Establish security protocols

Daily Meeting – this is primarily a working meeting

- Take minutes
- Document all issues
- Follow-up on open hotline issues
- Communicate findings, decisions and solutions to the team
- Do not get wrapped up in detail - schedule a new meeting to address specific issues
- Stop all "thrashing" sessions immediately

Weekly Progress Meeting

- ☐ Rotate minutes among the project team unless a scribe is assigned or volunteers
- ☐ Appropriate people attend
- ☐ Do not let the meeting become a problem resolution forum. Solve problems in a different meeting with the right people, not the whole team
- ☐ Individual reports and progress charts
- ☐ Visual progress charts
- ☐ Weekly status to team – Project Manager
- ☐ Weekly status report to Project Champion
- ☐ Schedule a specific update on all of the data conversion efforts
- ☐ If data conversion starts to run late, elevate the problem and fix it immediately

Monthly Progress Reports as Scheduled to the Appropriate Distribution List:

- ☐ Executive Champion
- ☐ Steering Committee
- ☐ President/CEO
- ☐ Board of Directors
- ☐ Associates

Policies, Procedures and Systems Documentation

- ☐ Option to use an outside technical writer – may be expensive
- ☐ New processes will make the maps used to analyze the system obsolete
- ☐ Updating the process maps may be simpler if a business process mapping program was used at the beginning of the project
- ☐ Document units of measure and quantities per assembly
- ☐ Document commodity codes
- ☐ Document salesperson and territory codes
- ☐ Document company and multi-plant codes

- ☐ Document the model and part number schemes
- ☐ User's manual for all new processes and how to use the systems
- ☐ Flows
- ☐ Screen prints
- ☐ Problem resolution methodologies
- ☐ Document systems changes

User Manuals

- ☐ Build user manuals for all processes / online, hardcopy, or both
  - ☐ Flow charts
  - ☐ Process Maps
  - ☐ Screen prints
  - ☐ Problem resolution methodologies
  - ☐ Document all systems changes

Use Temporary Help

- ☐ Free internal resources
- ☐ Speed up file building

Train

- ☐ Executives must make people available
- ☐ All training must be done with real data
- ☐ Training must be in sync with modules implemented
- ☐ End associates
- ☐ Technical personnel
- ☐ Create systems documentation and test the procedures
- ☐ Review and validate documentation – test by running process to document
- ☐ Technical support
- ☐ Hardware and software technical training must support the ERP system - if timed properly, it should not significantly delay the project, but it is required

- ☐ Do not move forward unless training is completed for a specific section

Test, Test, Test

- ☐ Test scripts prepared by associates
- ☐ Desired vs. probable result
- ☐ Unit test
- ☐ Tests by the end associates
    - ☐ Usability
    - ☐ Functionality
    - ☐ Expand testing to all associates in the department – module by module
- ☐ Take corrective actions immediately
- ☐ Do parallel testing to ensure quality
- ☐ Where parallel not possible, do pilot
- ☐ Systems test
    - ☐ Functionality
    - ☐ Networks
    - ☐ Security
    - ☐ Backup and restore
    - ☐ Disaster recovery

Go Live

Create "Go-Live" checklists clearly spelling out responsibilities and contingency plans.

Bring the team together and coordinate the conversion. Provide detailed work schedules. Remind all consultants this is a working session and they need to be there. Anyone can check data and help to exchange paperwork, including consultants.

Check the reports, both online and hard copy, and the new system to the old. Check detail line information as well as totals.

Sign off on systems acceptance. If someone refuses, find out the problem and fix it before going live. While people are cautious, they may have a good reason to delay the implementation. Listen to them, enlist them, and fix the problem, but make sure progress continues.

As identified earlier, files not programmatically converted require data entry, and the appropriate personnel must be available. Start manual conversion processes as early as possible.

Immediate Problem Resolution

Project leaders and consultants are responsible for problem resolution and are required to be on-site during the conversion process. All members of the conversion team will help fix problems.

Make sure help-line support is available, and calls promptly made and answered. Project Leadership must determine who can use the hotline. The user community has the need and right to expect fast answers and solutions. Management expects each one of them to be able to do their job, and they are highly justified to insist on good working tools from the vendor project team. The user community, in turn, must focus time and energy to problem resolution.

Record All Reported Problems

The team reviews the critical processes and paperwork (may be electronic images). These include inventory records, orders, invoices, accounts payable, shop paperwork, and picking lists.

The financial system requires exceptional attention. Taking a pre-implementation physical allows the validation of balances and facilitates spot-checking and correcting inventory balances. The sub ledgers and general ledger must be accurate. Review all problems and correct immediately, otherwise, they may snowball into the monthly financial statements, causing them to be late or inaccurate. Temporary workarounds are often required but make sure they are temporary. Incorporate the resolution into the future VMP, and fix them.

The system will still have bugs. The entire user community can help find and fix them.

Whoops

There are instances in the ERP world where the first reaction in the face of implementation problems is to go back to the old system. In the majority of cases, this is an overreaction. However, it is normal. This is where the executive champion and the project team leader must remain calm, logical, and provide the appropriate direction to the team.

While the Post-implementation stage is frequently stressful, the business can operate with some non-critical system deficiencies. That is the criteria for deciding whether to proceed or reverse actions, potentially causing as many problems as fixing the problem areas and moving ahead. Each company faced with this choice will have to make their own decision. If all the process steps were correctly completed, and the team is ready for some anticipated firefighting duties, they will probably be able to overcome any startup problems.

Step 8 Measure Post Operational State

ERP systems are complex and even with complete procedures and execution, testing all conditions and combinations is difficult. Anticipate multiple types of post implementation problems, ranging from simple to fix to showstoppers.

- Hardware and ERP issues
- Inaccurate procedures
- Operational problems
- Process changes
- Reports will not have the data expected
- Inadequate training

Problems are frequently in the seams, where information passes from one module to another. Middleware or other integration methodologies can increase the complexity of trouble shooting. Frequent errors occur in data mapping, resulting in information showing incorrectly, or using the wrong fields in the calculation. The use of proper testing and sign off procedures reduces errors. Post implementation problems are precisely the reason for doing weekend implementations. Start any conversion activities in advance, if they do not affect the business.

Post implementation issues often unfold over time, contrary to specifically around the implementation itself. Be patient and address each as soon as possible.

Ongoing

One of the implementation problems is the failure to communicate how much some jobs will change. Associates may have been doing the same thing for a number of years, but come to work on Monday morning, to a changed workplace, performing work differently. While trained, they may suffer lost feelings while working with the new system.

Those of us who engaged in project management are aware of how much change makes associates insecure. Management and supervision must be prepared to spend soft time with associates, reinforcing the new procedures, work rules, and methods. Additional training may be required. Provide it in good humor.

After the implementation follow up with each user and make sure they know precisely how to use the system. Take time to solve any problems they may be having.

Follow-Up

The system was justified based on certain expectations and anticipated return on investment. If ROI was justified:

- Using inventory turns - measure inventory turnover
- Using headcount reduction-measure actual jobs identified and those reduced
- Using Cash cycle reduction - measure the cash cycle

These measurements occur with predetermined frequency and consistency. Review the results with the management staff and the Board of Directors if required. Post them on the bulletin board and on-line project web site.

Immediately implement an auditing procedure for inventory and financial transactions. All financial reports must cross foot to legacy data and be carefully scrutinized.

Start user surveys. It is the responsibility of executive champion, team leader, and consultant to walk through the operation at least daily and talk to the people doing the work. They will take some justified criticism, but it is unfair and cowardly to hide in the office and hope that problems will magically disappear.

Management must listen to and involve the team. Members can help resolve problems or explain conflicting situations. The user community will take extraordinary steps to make the system a success when positively involved. Ignore the user community at peril. They are after all, the customers. In time, surveys can replace the daily walk.

If the system fails to meet expectations, internal and external, project leadership must explain why they have failed and provide options to improve the situation. This is the moment for final accountability.

Conduct post implementation lessons learned sessions with all the team members, consultants, and executive sponsor. Dissect how the problems were resolved. Discuss remaining problems, their status, and solutions. Have the consultants document unresolved issues and brief the project team. It signals the end of a Big-Bang ERP project, and moving to the next step for phased rollouts.

Personnel evaluation

Take the time for employee performance evaluations. Who were the stars? Who has demonstrated potential? Who are the candidates for development? You owe the team an honest evaluation.

Celebration

An ERP project is long and arduous, involving the extraordinary effort of management and associates. The members of the project team deserve special recognition in some form: a dinner/picnic with the executive staff, new leather coats, or a weekend at a resort for their families. Another type of celebration is catering a lunch or picnic as a thank you to all employees. A better idea is to do something special for your team plus the lunch. Following one team effort, the company had a picnic for the families, with a ritual burning of a few hardcopy reports from the old system.

The methods are varied and dependent on the culture of the business. The important thing is to celebrate the completion in a positive way. It may also be one way to start a culture change in the business as it uses new work tools to beat the competition.

The celebration step is easy to forget but the enterprise should reap huge returns using the new system. It is only fair to share with the people who made it happen. In addition, the next step in this process is to implement a value management program of some form. The executives of the enterprise will be asking and expecting many team members to take leadership roles in this effort, increasing pressure on operations. Reward the effort and fund the future.

Summary

- Measure performance
- Compare results to expectations
- Make adjustments where necessary
- Metrics -the system is providing the required functionality as planned.
- Achieving ROI is the next step.
- Share the rewards with the project team and organization
- Recognize the team

Congratulations

Step 9 Continuous Improvements - Perfect the System

It is time to "show me the money." When the core project is completed, the timing may be right for a project continuum. The objective is to perfect the system by changing and squeezing the waste out of all new business processes.

There are reasons for this approach.

The organization has already undergone some process improvement training. If it has been a full-blown business transformation program, training has been comprehensive, placing the enterprise in an excellent position to move forward.

Teams have successfully completed a complex project. The team members for a process improvement program may be different from those required for the ERP system, but in most organizations, some of the ERP members will play an active role in productivity programs.

The organization has learned how to function without the full-time involvement of many key team members. This does not mean exploiting members who sacrificed additional hours and made commitments to the ERP project. Do not expect the same time commitment with a new program. People will perform at a high level for a short-range project. Develop compensation or reward systems for long-term improvement programs, for example, a gain-sharing package.

For many companies, the decision will be to take a different path than VMP. This may be a new program such as supply-chain, CRM, a warehouse management program, or some other change process. While there will be pain in the transition, it is important to ride the momentum and reap the rewards.

Following is the Affinity Systems LLC "ACTION" methodology for VMP.

ACTION Methodology

ACTION is a synthesis of multiple thinking and problem solving methodologies.

Analyze

Use situational analysis to increase the awareness, define, and isolate opportunities for improvements.

- Separate situations from the background
- Bring components sharply into focus

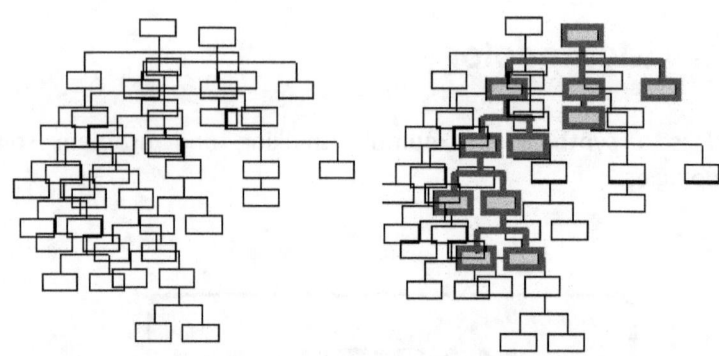

After the target identification is complete:

- Quantify the issue
- Test your interpretation

Ask:

- Is it a real problem?
- Does it justify an additional study?
- Is it small enough to make the change simple?
- Must the solution wait for a formal process?
- Is it critical, if yes take appropriate action?

Cause

Perform a root cause analysis to identify the true cause of the problem. Following are the principles for getting at the truth.

- Define the problem in writing
- Gather evidence

- Illustrate in visual terms – flowchart, photograph, illustration, video
- State in mathematical terms if possible
- Separate the symptoms from the problems
- Ask if it is a real problem
- Document the problem and the systems it feeds (Input-process-output)
- Document who does it and how the work is performed
- Work through each layer up and down, ask 'WHY' multiple times to get to the root cause
- Document obvious solutions and alternatives
- Make sure the problem is worth solving
- Define the impact on performance and think through possible unintended consequences
- Define the impact on revenue stream
- Define impact on corporate values
- Define the impact on the mission
- Additional definition may be required to gain proper focus

Think

Analyze the problem and potential solutions. Apply the principles for thinking to develop, and test future state solutions. Work beyond the obvious and the quick fix

- Overcome bias
- Force yourself to get information that may prove you wrong
- Acquire additional knowledge
- Use tools for problem solving
- Seek expert opinion
- Research – if and how was this problem solved before (perhaps in a different environment or industry)
- Collaborative evaluation
- Team evaluation of evidence, cause and effect
- Analyze a problem in reverse
- Extrapolate a solution – can you backfill facts and logic

- Defeat path most traveled (fixation)
- Define how to make the solution visual
- Attempt to disprove the solution
- Test solution with customer
- Experiment
- Critical review
- Ask what if, why not and so what
- Think through consequences of potential solutions
- Make a decision to fix, ignore or postpone problem resolution

Problem solving is granular, which works in both directions, viewing the problem through a microscope or telescope. Change the perspective.

Break all the observations into time elements.

Innovate

Innovation is a trained process. It follows a simple format. There must first be knowledge, followed by creativity, then thinking and finally, innovation. Enlightened governance sets the team free to work the magic.

The steps to innovation are:

- Process knowledge
- Curiosity

- Thinking and analyzing
- Collaboration and networking
- Trial and error
- Positive results
- Honest feedback
- Test solution
- Communicate to all involved
- Implement solutions
- Measure
- Correct and re-test if necessary

Ownership

Correctly done, ownership starts and ends with the project team. Make sure there are names on the project plan to identify champions, leaders, and team members. Develop a sense of priority and purpose across the team. Empower the team, so they own the project.

Following the implementation and correction of a new process, departmental personnel, individually and collectively, must take process ownership. Using the functional team approach, this step is nearly automatic. When management or consultants install the new process, this is a specific set of predefined actions.

- Operational state
- Ownership
- Follow-up
- Measurement is ongoing
- Keep looking for new opportunities to improve

Normalize

Once ownership is established and the team starts the documentation step, they will find ways to simplify and standardize the process.

Make the improvements stick by designating them "the way" until it is superseded with a new iteration. This step is necessary. It holds the gains and establishes a platform for future improvement, while creating a culture of quality and continuous improvement.

- Document and make the change transparent
- Simplify
- Standardize
- Communicate the new process and train as needed
- Continually measure the new way and improve as needed

Comparison to Lean Six Sigma

Following is a comparison of Lean Six Sigma and new ACTION. Use this as a checklist when reviewing PI programs.

	Lean Six Sigma	H-Lean
Strategy	Continuum	Continuum
Metrics	Right thing	Right thing
Information technology	Not integrated	Integrated
Purpose	Improve processes	Improve thinking
Objective	Improve process	Change process
Performance	Schedule	Now
Change philosophy	Iterative	Transformative
Area of focus	Process	System
Paradigm	Continuum	New continuum
Silo	Address	Integrate
Program structure	Leaders	Empowered teams
Program management	Lip service	Real
Management perspective	Thing to do	Must do
Change	Operational processes	Everything
Power	Structured	Team
Attitude	Ego	Ego-energy
Teams	Improve processes	Improve people
		Innovate
		Automate

Tools

Teach associates the appropriate tool usage. Not every participant needs to know how to use them all. There is a history of highly successful projects where the team members learned only flowcharting. As in every part of the project, it is important to determine what tools your team needs, and provide them. Some useful improvement tools are:

1. Check sheets
2. Flow charts
3. Operational definitions
4. Run chart
5. Capability analysis
6. Cause and effect diagrams
7. Force field analysis
8. Histograms
9. Nominal group techniques
10. Pareto diagrams
11. Affinity diagrams
12. Scatter diagrams
13. Sampling techniques
14. Control charts
15. Spread sheets
16. Facilitation skills
17. Change management models
18. Listening skills
19. Brainstorming (Intensive Planning)
20. Surveys
21. Collaboration techniques
22. Thinking tools

Summary

With the software installed and operational, one significant option is to shift efforts to a VMP.

- Process Improvement is nearly always required to meet the ROI.
- Title – Lean Six Sigma not important, only the RESULTS count.
- Concepts – VMP is another topic, but the basic concepts are:
    o Eliminate non-value adding activities
    o Eliminate waste
    o Reduce variability
    o Compress time (increase velocity)
    o Simplify
    o Standardize

ACTION provides a different way to evaluate and solve problems. Since the intent of this book is to provide a fresh look at the development, deployment and operation of corporate resource management programs, we choose to use a condensed version of the method. The entire process will appear in later publications. Check competitiveamerica.us for availability.

Enjoy the process and celebrate the success.

About the Author

Wayne Staley established Affinity Systems LLC, a system consulting company, in 1997.

 An Army veteran and military Operating Room Technician, Wayne worked as an Emergency Room and X-Ray Technician in civilian institutions.

Later educated in computer technology and business systems, he has managed Corporate Information Technology, Materials, Logistics, and manufacturing.

He has shop floor experience as Manager of Shop Operations of a complex fabrication complex, which included a foundry. Wayne worked on integrated supply chain programs with China based suppliers, and collaboration programs with Dow Chemical and other customers.

He has managed numerous Business Strategy, Enterprise Resource Planning (ERP), and process improvement projects (VMP) in manufacturing, government, distribution, and convention management.

He developed training materials for ERP, Supply-Chain Management, Strategy, and Process Improvement. He created a graphic arts company, Phase Four Graphics, (phasefourgraphics.com), and CompetitiveAmerica.us, advocating for American industry.

His other books are:

Pathway to Adaptability - 2008
Crunch Time for Health care - 2011
ERP Information at the Speed of Reality - 2013
Productivity Prescriptions for Health Care - 2014

ERP Information at the Speed of Reality

Wayne L Staley

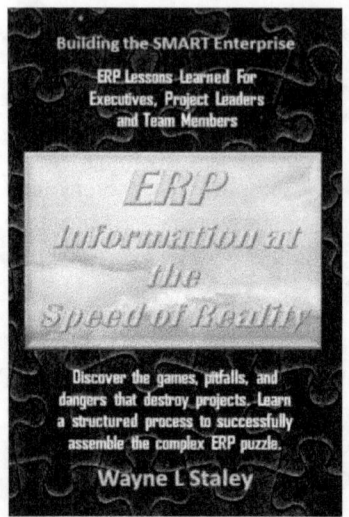

Building the SMART Enterprise

ERP Lessons-Learned For
Executives, Project Leaders
and Team Members

ERP

Information at

the

Speed of Reality

Discover the games, pitfalls, and
dangers that destroy projects. Learn
a structured process to successfully
assemble the complex ERP puzzle.

Wayne L Staley

Information reality

Every type of business must execute effectively and move from a physical and information reality of weeks and days to minutes and seconds. The smart enterprise builds intelligence gathering in near real time, taking full advantage of faster operations.

The games people play

Consultants, executives, project leaders, software suppliers all play games that introduce unnecessary variables into a complex process. We share our experience of forty-five years because it will help businesses to succeed. Some stories are enlightening, but not funny because companies, their employees, and ownership paid the price.

Due diligence

Ignorance is not bliss, excusable or acceptable. Discover the truth – think beyond the obvious and overcome ignorance with education and training. Major project pitfalls are assumptions, bias, and fixation.

Assemble the puzzle

ERP projects are complex, involving strategies, internal assessments, evaluation of multiple alternatives, and making critical business decisions. They require assigning high performers to project teams, taking them away from important daily activities. ERP systems are so expensive that failure is not an option. Evidence based decisions and a structured process lead to successful results.

Pathway to Adaptability

Wayne L Staley

"If you don't know where you're going, any path will take you there."

The Cheshire cat

Alice's Wonderland is a labyrinth filled with strange places, unusual ideas, unexpected occupants, and unpredictable events. One danger is running ever faster but staying in the same place, a clear sign of lost direction.

This description applies to the real business world but even more volatile and unforgiving forces' sort it all out – the marketplace. It demands the correct products, appropriately priced and available now. Speed is King!

Pathway to Adaptability is for corporate leaders, executives, managers, and administrators who govern businesses of all types.

In Pathway to Adaptability, you will travel on an eight-step pathway through the corporate alignment process. The book provides assessments to track your progress.

Enterprises must become very smart, building real-time intelligence into every activity. Without accurate information foundations, and process improvement, adaptability is not achievable and significant opportunities will be lost.

"This book has invaluable information on LEAN Six Sigma Methodology that is used in my company, and has been used as a reference point in many of our LEAN Focus Groups across the country. I highly recommend Wayne Staley's book." Amazon review by Black Belt

Get Pathway to Adaptability at -http://www.competitiveamerica.us, Amazon.co. - Also available in Kindle.

Productivity Prescriptions for Health Care

Wayne L Staley and Jon Bingol

Productivity Prescriptions for Health Care

Patient Centric
Process Improvement

Wayne Staley and Jon Bingol

The primary mission of health care professionals, executive leadership, and associates is delivering quality health care to patients. The past model was doctor/patient, but numerous new wedges were driven between the two, adding complexity and cost.

The ACA, passed in 2010, created a new health care model, and transformation is proving difficult and expensive. Compliance puts many health care organizations in a financial bind. One of the most powerful tools to address operational problems is process improvement programs.

Crunch Time for Health Care, written before the resolution of sundry challenges to the ACA, contained discussions regarding the viability and implications of the law. With the issues settled and Health care focused on compliance, a refreshed manuscript was required.

Productivity Prescriptions for Health Care provides a structured program methodology for defining and implementing contemporary programs specifically designed for the special requirements of health care organizations.

To the practitioners of Lean, Health care is a special calling. Nothing parallels the heart-breaking experience of watching life fade while working frantically to preserve it. The thought that process improvement potentially makes life saving tools less accessible, is repugnant and immoral. We have created a special symbol as a constant reminder, life trumps efficiency.

Productivity improvement programs are required for future Health care sustainability, with quality and efficiency the twins for success.

Crunch Time for Health Care

Wayne L Staley and Jon Bingol

Continuous Process Improvement for the Medical Profession

CRUNCH TIME For **Health Care**

People are the competitive advantage

H-LEAN

Wayne Staley and Jon Bingol

Time is running out for health care, as we know it

Dramatic changes in the health care system are causing paradigm shifts in patient care. While the intent was to improve quality, the cost of medical care is still unchecked and profitability is suffering.

Time is life

Medical care must embrace patient-centered process improvement such as reducing the "door to balloon" time. An example is moving the 12 lead EKG from the emergency room to the ambulance, allowing the patient to go directly to the cath lab.

Current and future patients need this information to help them make informed medical decisions in the new world of healthcare.

Time is Money

H-Lean is a concept designed around health care. Every person in the industry will be involved in or affected by the dramatic changes. This book will help you become more knowledgeable, allowing you to participate through positive ACTION.

Get Crunch Time for Health Care at -http://www.competitiveamerica.us, Amazon.co. - Also available in Kindle.

Bibliography

The Production Information Control System   IBM
MRPII Unlocking America's Productivity Potential
                                    Oliver W. Wight
Business Simulation   CMS manufacturing Systems
Tying the Shop Floor to the ERP System Plex Systems
10 Famous ERP Disasters, Dustups, and Disappointments
                                    Thomas Wailgum, CIO
Successful ERP Implementations the First Time
                                    R. Michael Donovan
Top 15 ERP Software Vendors Revealed 2010
                                    Business-Software.com
ERP Software-Implementation Best Practices
                                    Pollyanne S. Frantz
                                    Arthur R. Southerland
                                    James T. Johnson
Enterprise Resource Planning – Factors Affecting Success and Failure
                                    Patricia Barton
The Essential Guide for Selecting Todays Business Software
                                    SoftResources
                                    John Adams
                                    Richard Dance
                                    Joe Kersey
                                    Trisha Tubba
Top 15 ERP Software Vendors Revealed-2010 Edition
                                    Business-Software.com
Selecting an ERP Solution: A Guide   INFOR
11 Criteria for Selecting the Best ERP System Replacement
                                    EPICOR
The Next Generation of ERP Software   David A. Turbide-EPICOR
Rapid Implementation: The New Age of Oracle
                                    Mindy Blodgett
ERP/EDI Integration Methodologies – In-house vs. Hosted
                                    John   Simmons-
                                    www.dicentral.com

Best Practices in Extending ERP   Aberdeen Group
Executive Guide to Business and Software Requirements
                                         Keith Ellis
                                         IAG Consulting
Midmarket/Enterprise ERP Solutions Comparison Guide
                                         FOCUS
ERP Systems Market Guide   FOCUS
Essential Features of Manufacturing ERP Software
                                         Scott Priestley
                                         FOCUS
The Fifth Discipline   Peter Senge
Lateral Thinking for Management   Edward de Bono
The 2010 Meltdown   Edward E. Gordon
Leadership and the New Science   Margaret J. Wheatley
Thriving on Chaos   Tom Peters
Complex Organizations   Amitai Etzioni
The Change Agent   Lee Grossman
Consilience: The Unity of Knowledge   Edward o. Wilson
Performance Consulting – Moving Beyond Training
                                         Dana Gaines Robinson
                                         James C. Robinson
Complexity – The Emerging Science at the Edge of Order and Chaos
                                         M. Mitchell Waldrop
Leadership and the New Science: Learning about Organization from an
Orderly Universe   Margaret J. Wheatley
Successful Management by Objectives   Karl Albrecht
Liberation Management   Tom Peters
The Machine That Changed the World   James Womack
                                         Daniel Jones
                                         Daniel Roos
The 13 Secrets of Power Performance   Roger Dawson
Value Migration   Adrian J. Slywotzky
The Mind of the Strategist   Kenichi Ohmae
The Rise and Fall of Strategic Planning   Henry Mintzberg
The Fifth Discipline: The Art and Practice of the Learning Organization
                                         Peter Senge
The 7 Habits of Highly Effective People   Stephen R. Covey

The New Rules   John P. Cotter
Leading Change   John P. Cotter
Crossing the Chasm   Geoffrey A. Moore
Top Management Strategy What it is and How to Make It Work
                                       Benjamin B. Tregoe
                                       John W. Zimmerman
  The Theory of Inventive Problem Solving
                                     www.mazur.net/triz/
40 Principles-TRIZ Keys to Technical Innovation
                                     Genrich Atschuller
One Minute Manager   Kenneth Blanchard, PhD
                                     Spencer Johnson, MD
To Err is Human: Building a Safer Health System
                                     Institute of Medicine
MRPII Unlocking America's Productivity Potential
                                     Oliver W. Wight
What the CEO Wants You to Know   Ram Charan
High Velocity Leadership   Brian K. Muirhead
                                     William L. Simon
Lean Thinking   James   P.   Womack
                                     Daniel T. Jones
The Frontiers of Management   Peter Drucker
The Handbook of Strategic Expertise Catherine Hayden
Quality is Free   Philip B. Crosby
Kanban – Just In Time at Toyota   Edited by Japan Management
                                   Association
The Japanese Art of War   Thomas Cleary
It's Not Luck   Eliyahu M. Goldratt
Bionomics: Economy as Ecosystem   Michael Rothschild
Business at the Speed of Thought   Bill Gates
Theory of Constraints   Eliyahu M. Goldratt
The Goal   Eliyahu M. Goldratt
                                   Jeff Cox
How to Manage Change Effectively   Donald L. Kirkpatrick
Technology, Management and Society Peter F. Drucker
Performance Consulting –Moving Beyond Training
                                   Dana Gaines Robinson

	James C. Robinson
Lightning Strategies for Innovation	Willard L. Zangwill
CRM at The Speed of Light	Paul Greenberg
The Reengineering Revolution	Michael Hammer
Beyond Reengineering	Michael Hammer
World Class Manufacturing-The Lessons of Simplicity Applied	
	Richard J. Schonberger
Computer Applications in Manufacturing	
	Thomas G. Gunn
Best Practices – Building Your Business With Customer Focused Solution	
	Robert Hiebeler
	Thomas B. Kelly
	Charles Ketterman
Solving Business Problems by Simulation	
	Jan Szymankiewicz
	James McDonald
	Keith Turner
Customer Centered Growth-Five Strategies for Building Competitive Advantage	Richard Whiteley
	Diane Hessan
Inside Teams – How 20 World-Class Organizations are Winning Through Teamwork	Richard S. Wellins
	William C. Byham
	George R. Dixon
Supply Chain Development for the Lean Enterprise	
	Robin Cooper
	Regine Slagmulder
The Concept of Corporate Strategy	Kenneth R. Andrews
Complexity and the Experience of Leading Organizations	
	Edited By Douglas Griffin
	Ralph Stacey
The Art of Innovation	Tom Kelly
	Jonathan Littman
Principle Centered Leadership	Steven R. Covey
Predicting the Future of Business	Wayne Rash
Future Tech: Where Will ERP Be in 2 Years?	
	inside-erp.com

Your Strategic Guide to Converged Infrastructure
                              Bob Violino
Breakthrough Thinking – The Seven Principles of Creative Problem
                              Solving Gerald Nader, PhD
                              Shozo Hibini, PhD
                              John Farrell
Great Leaders Grow: Becoming A Leader for Life
                              Kenneth Blanchard
                              Mark MIller
Systematic Innovation: An Introduction to Triz
                              John Terninko
                              Alla Zusman
                              Boris Zlotin
Toolbox   Wwww.toolbox.com
APICS (The Association for Operations Management)
                              www.apics.org
Aberdeen Group   www.aberdeen.com
WWW.Technology Evaluation. Com
Private Cloud ERP in a Hybrid Cloud   Oracle Corp.
SaaS versus on-premise ERP   Ziff Davis B2B
A SaaS Primer   PLEX
The Real SaaS Manifesto: Defining "Real SaaS" and how it can benefit
your business   Workday, Inc.
Best Practices for Managing Just-in-Time (JIT) Production
                              Richard Bird
                              Jerry Durant
                              Michele Tomasicchio
                              Lonnie Wilson
Changing the Way Business Intelligence Is Managed
                              SAP
Business Growing Pains? How to Tell When You Need a Modern ERP
Solution   Sage North America
Mobility in Consumer Products   *Simon* Ellis
Best of Breed vs Integrated Systems   Online Consultant Software
A Smarter Path to ERP Selection   Compare Business Products
The 2011 Focus Experts' Guide to Enterprise Resource Planning
                              Michael Krigsman

5 Advantages to Using Industry specific software
                                    VISCO
IBM Sterling Supply Chain Visibility   IBM Corporation
Magic Quadrants and Market Scopes: How Gartner Evaluates Vendors
Within a Market   Gartner
Lessons from ERP Implementation Failures